"The wild and unscholarly yet widely accepted assertion by Richard Dawkins that the only difference between *The Da Vinci Code* and the Gospels is that the Gospels are ancient fiction while *The Da Vinci Code* is modern fiction deserves a measured and scholarly response. There is no one better qualified than Peter Williams to provide it, and this book is a masterly presentation of a compelling cumulative case that 'all of history hangs on Jesus.'"

John C. Lennox, Emeritus Professor of Mathematics, University of Oxford

"This much-needed book provides a mine of information for Christians wanting to know more about the historical background to the Gospels and offers a series of challenges to those skeptical of what we can know about Jesus. Peter Williams has distilled a mass of information and thought into this short and accessible book, and it deserves careful reading both inside and outside the church."

Simon Gathercole, Reader in New Testament Studies, University of Cambridge

"Despite the doctrine of biblical inerrancy, Christians today find themselves unwilling to testify to their faith, as much from confusion as from fear. To this puzzled, anxious flock, Peter Williams offers liberation in the form of a concise yet complete education. His powerful instruction manual on the reliability of the Gospels escorts the 'faithful seeking understanding' through a series of historically responsible explanations for questions they have and questions they never imagined. This highly detailed, accurate, and eminently readable volume—rich in charts and tables—strikes a chord so resonant, Christians and skeptics alike can profit. An up-to-date apologia and superlative guide—unbelievers, beware!"

Clare K. Rothschild, Professor of Scripture Studies, Lewis University; author, *Luke-Acts and the Rhetoric of History*; *Baptist Traditions and Q*; and *Hebrews as Pseudepigraphon*; Editor, *Early Christianity*

"With his expert knowledge and skill, yet in a remarkably easy-to-follow way, Williams, one of the world's leading authorities on the text of the New Testament, takes the reader through various lines of evidence supporting the historical reliability of the Gos~~~~. This ~~~~~~~~~~~~~~~~~ is rational to trust the Gospels."

Edward Adams, Professor of New Te~~~~~~ King's College London

Can We Trust the Gospels?

Can We Trust the Gospels?

Peter J. Williams

:: CROSSWAY®

WHEATON, ILLINOIS

Trade paperback ISBN: 978-1-4335-5295-3
ePub ISBN: 978-1-4335-5295-7
PDF ISBN: 978-1-4335-5296-0
Mobipocket ISBN: 978-1-4335-5297-7

Library of Congress Cataloging-in-Publication Data

Names: Williams, Peter J., 1970– author.
Title: Can we trust the gospels? / Peter J. Williams.
Description: Wheaton, Illinois: Crossway, [2018] | Includes bibliographical references and index.
Identifiers: LCCN 2018016921 (print) | LCCN 2018021786 (ebook) | ISBN 9781433552960 (pdf) | ISBN 9781433552977 (mobi) | ISBN 9781433552984 (epub) | ISBN 9781433552953 (tp)
Subjects: LCSH: Jesus Christ—Historicity. | Bible. Gospels—Evidences, authority, etc.
Classification: LCC BT303.2 (ebook) | LCC BT303.2 .W49 2018 (print) | DDC 226/.01—dc23
LC record available at https://lccn.loc.gov/2018016921

Crossway is a publishing ministry of Good News Publishers.

BP		33	32	31	30	29	28	27	26	25	24	23
21	20	19	18	17	16	15	14	13	12	11	10	9

For my parents-in-law,
David and Joan Eeley

Contents

Illustrations

Tables

Figure

Preface

I have long felt the need for a short book explaining to a general audience some of the vast amount of evidence for the trustworthiness of the four Gospels. There are various great treatments of this topic, and each book has its own focus.[1] This one seeks to present a case for the reliability of the Gospels to those who are thinking about the subject for the first time. I could have made the book far longer by giving more examples and references or by considering objections, but for the sake of brevity I have cut out everything unnecessary. I have sought to give enough information for interested readers to check the evidence, but I have generally avoided referring to the literally millions of pages of New Testament scholarship, of which I have read only the tiniest part.

I have many people to thank for various forms of help, including advice, critical comment, encouragement, financial support, proofreading, research assistance, and technical expertise. Professor Richard Bauckham, James Bejon, Rich and Carrie Berg, Phillip and Kathleen Evans, Dr. Simon Gathercole, Julian

---

1. My top recommendations are Charles E. Hill, *Who Chose the Gospels? Probing the Great Gospel Conspiracy* (Oxford: Oxford University Press, 2010); Lydia McGrew, *Hidden in Plain View: Undesigned Coincidences in the Gospels and Acts* (Chillicothe, OH: DeWard, 2017); Brant Pitre, *The Case for Jesus: The Biblical and Historical Evidence for Christ* (New York: Image, 2016); and at greater length, Craig L. Blomberg, *The Historical Reliability of the New Testament* (Nashville: B&H Academic, 2016).

Hardyman, Jack Haughton, Dr. John Hayward, Dr. Martin Heide, Peter Hunt, Dr. David Instone-Brewer, Dr. Dirk Jongkind, Mark and Becky Lanier, Kevin Matthews, Peter Montoro, Phil and Judy Nussbaum, Philip and Helen Page, Lily Rivers, Laura Robinson, Professor Rodney Sampson, Anna Stevens, Julie Woodson, and Dr. Lorne Zelyck have all assisted in some way in the production of this book, as have the Tyndale House staff and trustees. I am also grateful to family members Diana, Kathryn, Magdalena, and Leo Williams for their support and critical comment. It has been a pleasure to write this book within the setting of Tyndale House in Cambridge, whose library some regard as the best place on earth for conducting biblical research. Many thanks must go to my friends at Crossway for their extraordinary work in publication.

Introduction

It is common today to speak of *world faiths* or to describe some people as having faith, as if others do not. Faith is seen as a non-rational belief—something not based on evidence. However, that is not what faith originally meant for Christians. Coming from the Latin word *fides*, the word *faith* used to mean something closer to our word *trust*. Trust, of course, can be based on evidence.

This book's title, *Can We Trust the Gospels?*, is therefore carefully chosen. It addresses the question by looking at evidence of the Gospels' trustworthiness. The great thing about trust is that it is something we all understand to a degree because we all exercise it.

Most of us regularly place our personal safety in the hands of others. We trust food suppliers, civil engineers, and car manufacturers literally with our lives. We also depend on friends, social media, and financial services. Of course, our trust is not absolute and unquestioning. If we see flagrant breaches of hygiene in a restaurant, we probably stop eating there. But trust is still something we exercise daily. We place qualified trust in news sources, both for information that affects our lives and for information that does not. It is a version of that everyday sort of trust that we are going to consider in this book as we ask whether we can trust the accounts of Jesus's life, namely, the four Gospels found in the second major part of the Bible, called the New Testament.

Trusting the Gospels is both the same as trusting other things and different. It is the same in that we often have to evaluate the credibility of people and things in daily life. It is different in that the Gospels contain accounts of miracles and of a man, Jesus Christ, who is presented as the supernatural Son of God who can rightfully claim ownership of our lives.[1] But before we consider such claims, we need to ask whether the Gospels show the signs of trustworthiness we usually look for in things we believe.

Of course, as we examine the Gospels, I would first encourage you to read them. You should be able to do that comfortably out loud in under nine hours. You might worry about which translation to use, but it makes little difference. If you find the Gospels of Matthew, Mark, Luke, and John online or in a printed Bible, you will probably have enough to make sense of this book.

---

1. Though the word *supernatural* may imply a gulf between a mechanical natural order and a supernatural realm, I do not mean to imply anything more here than that the Gospels relate miraculous events that are unparalleled in the daily experience of most people.

1

What Do Non-Christian Sources Say?

It is hardly surprising that Christian texts are our main source of information about the origins of Christianity. Most books on archery, baseball, or cooking are by enthusiasts of those activities. Christians were the most enthusiastic about Christianity and naturally wrote more about it. The four Gospels were, of course, written by advocates of belief in Jesus as the promised deliverer. They may therefore be said to be biased, in the sense that they are not impartial records but ones aiming to foster belief in Jesus Christ.

However, their bias does not mean we should distrust their record. An innocent man accused of a crime may have a deep interest in proving his innocence, but this bias is not a reason to dismiss evidence he produces. The question, then, is not whether the Gospel writers had an agenda, but whether they reported accurately.

Some sources, however, cannot be accused of bias in favor of Christianity. These include non-Christians who wrote within ninety years of the origins of Christianity and left us with records we can investigate. We will begin by considering three writers: Cornelius Tacitus, Pliny the Younger, and Flavius Josephus. Each of these had his own reason for writing, but in no case was it the promotion of Christianity. Tacitus and Pliny were, in fact, openly hostile to Christianity.

Cornelius Tacitus

Tacitus was born around the year AD 56. He held a series of distinguished Roman offices, including being a senator and a consul. He is now most famed for his writings, which include those shown in table 1.1.[1]

Table 1.1. Writings of Tacitus

Short Title	Content	Length	Approximate Date
Agricola	About Tacitus's father-in-law, Julius Agricola, governor of Britain, including a description of Britain and its people	1 book	AD 98
Germania	A description of Rome's dealings with the Germanic tribes	1 book	AD 98
Histories	A narrative of Roman history covering the years AD 69–96	14 books	AD 109
Annals	A narrative of Roman history covering the years AD 14–68	16 books	AD 115–117

Tacitus certainly had biases. He recounted history in order to give moral instruction, praising those he approved of and often applying a whole armory of rhetorical strategies to damn those he disliked. However, his ability to record factual information is first-rate. He could accurately describe remote places he had never visited and was the first to provide literature on

---

1. Tacitus may also have written the *Dialogue on Oratory*, which has a somewhat different style.

the lochs in Scotland. He appears to have had access to sources that allowed him to relate detailed stories from more than four decades before he was born.[2] We therefore have little reason to doubt the broad facts underlying his account of the early Christians as found in his *Annals*. To quote the *Oxford Companion to Classical Literature*, "The *Annals* in particular show Tacitus to have been one of the greatest of historians, with a penetrating insight into character and a sober grasp of the significant issues of the time."[3]

Tacitus wrote about the Great Fire in Rome, which occurred in July AD 64. He told of how it was thought that the mad emperor Nero had started the fire and yet blamed the many Christians then in Rome, accusing them of arson. In his career in Rome, Tacitus would have been able to talk to many adults about its events and to have access to Rome's official records. We therefore have every reason to treat the outline of facts he provides as reliable.

This is how Tacitus tells the story, using the common early spelling of *Christians* as *Chrestians*:[4]

---

2. See Ronald Syme, "Tacitus: Some Sources of His Information," *The Journal of Roman Studies* 72 (1982): 68–82.

3. M. C. Howatson, ed., *The Oxford Companion to Classical Literature*, 2nd ed. (Oxford: Oxford University Press, 1997), 548.

4. The oldest manuscript of this passage, Codex Laurentianus Mediceus 68.2, has *Chrestianos*, which a later scribe has corrected to *Christianos* (accusative plural of *Christianus*). The spelling with *e* rather than *i* is extremely common in early centuries, but Tacitus learnedly states that while the "crowd" called the group *Chrestiani*, with *e*, the correct origin of the name was from *Christus*, with *i*. There is continual evidence of vowel confusion for the centuries following Tacitus. Justin Martyr (*First Apology* 4), writing in Greek to the Roman emperor Antoninus Pius in the mid-second century, makes a play on the name Christian and the word "good" (*chrēstos*). Around AD 200, Tertullian, *Apology* 3, complains that opponents wrongly call Christians *Chrestiani*. At the beginning of the fourth century, Lactantius, *Divine Institutions* 4.7, notes that Latin speakers sometimes mistakenly call Christ *Chrēstus*. In biblical manuscripts, although the spelling of Christ and Christian with *i* is attested early (see manuscript TM 61617 for *Christos*, and Papyrus 72 at 1 Peter 4:16 for *Christianos*), it is not clearly in a majority before the fifth century, especially since the name *Christ* is usually spelled in New Testament manuscripts as an abbreviation, which does not reveal the vowel. Though Greek pronunciation was also shifting, there is plenty of evidence from before the fifth century for the use of vowels other than Greek *iota*, which was the normal representation of an *i* sound. Codex

But neither human help, nor gifts from the emperor, nor all the ways of placating Heaven, could stifle scandal or dispel the belief that the fire had taken place by order [of Nero]. Therefore, to scotch the rumour, Nero substituted as culprits, and punished with the utmost refinements of cruelty, a class of men, loathed for their vices, whom the crowd called *Chrestians*. Christus, the founder of the name, had undergone the death penalty in the reign of Tiberius, by sentence of the procurator Pontius Pilatus, and the pernicious superstition was checked for a moment, only to break out once more, not merely in Judaea, the home of the disease, but in the capital [Rome] itself, where all things horrible or shameful in the world collect and become fashionable. First, then, the confessed members of the sect were arrested; next, on their disclosures, vast numbers were convicted, not so much on the count of arson as for hatred of the human race. And derision accompanied their end: they were covered with wild beasts' skins and torn to death by dogs; or they were fastened on crosses, and, when daylight failed were burned to serve as lamps by night. Nero had offered his Gardens for the spectacle, and gave an exhibition in his Circus, mixing with the crowd in the clothes of a charioteer, or mounted on his chariot. Hence, in spite of a guilt which

---

Vaticanus and Codex Sinaiticus (both fourth century) are the earliest manuscripts for the three New Testament occurrences of the term *Christian* (Acts 11:26; 26:28; 1 Peter 4:16). Vaticanus has *Chreistianos* (Greek, χρειστιανος), and Sinaiticus has *Chrēstianos* (Greek, χρηστιανος). Vaticanus also spells *antichrist* and *pseudochrist* with *ei* (ει) and uses *ei* on the two occasions when it spells out the name *Christ* in full (see Matthew 24:24; Mark 13:22; 2 Corinthians 10:7; 1 Peter 1:11; 1 John 2:18, 22; 4:3; 2 John 7). The form with *eta* is the main spelling in the earliest Coptic versions of the New Testament. The close alignment of *iota* and *eta* allows Greek word play on the word "good" (*chrestos*) and the word "Christ" (*Christos*) in 1 Peter 2:3. Some scholars distinguish the group mentioned in Tacitus from the later Christians, but this ignores widespread evidence for the vowel interchange in Latin and Greek and involves supposing that Tacitus was gravely confused. It also does not explain why Suetonius, *Life of Nero* 16, calls a group Nero punished at this time *Christiani*. Moreover, it invents an otherwise unattested group called the *Chrestiani*, who are present in Rome in large numbers and are persecuted at a time and in ways that later Christians remembered they were persecuted. These hypothetically widespread *Chrestiani* then disappear off the globe.

had earned the most exemplary punishment, there arose a sentiment of pity, due to the impression that they were being sacrifices not for the welfare of the state but to the ferocity of a single man.[5]

The question should be raised how we know Tacitus actually wrote this. Is it not possible that the work of this pagan writer was tampered with by later Christian scribes? This has been the claim of a few scholars but has remained a marginal view for several reasons, of which I will give just two.

First, it should be remembered that *all* Greek and Latin literature transmitted to us from the classical period to the Middle Ages was handed down by *Christian* scribes. They preserved the references to Greek and Roman gods and faithfully copied religious ideas that differed from their own Christian views. In the last century or so, much-older manuscripts from before Christian times have been found in the dry sands of Egypt, and these show that scribes generally copied faithfully. The burden of proof is therefore on those who want to maintain that texts have been changed since classical times.

Second, Tacitus had a unique style of Latin, part of what is commonly called silver Latin, to distinguish it from Latin of the golden age of Cicero (107/106–43 BC). As every century passed, Latin changed, as all languages do. Medieval scribes were educated in medieval Latin and would not have been aware of all the differences between their own Latin and that of Tacitus. It would have been difficult for them to imitate Tacitus's style of Latin for more than a few phrases at the most. That is why classical scholars today treat this as a reliable account, at least in regard to the main events.

---

5. Tacitus, *Annals* 15.44. Translation lightly adapted for readability from *Tacitus Annals Books 13–16*, Loeb Classical Library 322 (Cambridge, MA: Harvard University Press, 1937), 283, 285. I have also adapted the translation to use the spelling *Chrestians* rather than *Christians*.

The narrative provides significant information. We obviously learn that Tacitus did not like Christians (he calls the religion a "disease"), and yet he helps us establish some useful facts. He uses the name *Christus*, the Latin word from which we get *Christ*. Tacitus regards Christus as the source of the name, and his followers were a group that others called *Chrestiani*, with the well-documented vulgar Latin substitution of *e* for *i*.[6] We note that Tacitus says it was the crowd who named them Chrestians, not the followers themselves. This fits with the three occurrences of the word *Christian* in the New Testament (Acts 11:26; 26:28; 1 Peter 4:16). The term was first applied by non-Christians and only later was adopted by Christians themselves.

Latin *Christus* is simply a transliteration of the Greek word *Christos*, which means "anointed" and is equivalent to the Hebrew word *Messiah*. As the Messiah was the promised deliverer whom many Jews were expecting, the name *Christian* tells us clearly of this group's belief that the promised Jewish deliverer had come. As we will see, Christianity arose in the cradle of Judaism, and the further back we go in time, the more Jewish all our records of Christianity are. This means we are able to guess certain elements of the beliefs of this group even without considering their writings.

We may also establish certain other things. Tacitus tells us that Christ was put to death while Tiberius was emperor, thus between AD 14 and AD 37. Tacitus also tells us that this happened while Pontius Pilate was in charge of Judaea, which was between AD 26 and AD 36. Tacitus thus gives us an approximate fixed point for the founding events of Christianity.

---

6. For evidence of the interchange of *e* and *i* see E. H. Sturtevant, *The Pronunciation of Greek and Latin: The Sounds and Accents* (Chicago: University of Chicago Press, 1920), 15–29, 120. It is common that initial contact with a group involves mispronunciation of their name, followed by subsequent correction. Thus in the West the less accurate spelling *Moslem* was only recently replaced by the more accurate spelling *Muslim*.

In addition to giving us this chronological framework, Tacitus helps us with geographical information. He tells us that the "disease" named after Christ started in Judaea, which is where all the Christian sources also claim Christianity started. Christian texts tell us that Jesus Christ was executed near Jerusalem, the spiritual center of Judaea. Tacitus tells us that at the time of the Great Fire in AD 64, there were many Christians in Rome. He uses the Latin phrase *multitudo ingens*, "vast multitude." Christianity had clearly spread a long way, since the distance, as the crow flies, between Jerusalem and Rome is around 2,300 kilometers (1,430 miles), greater than the distance between Edinburgh and the north of Morocco, or between New York City and Havana.

Tacitus also explains how Nero treated the Christians cruelly and many of them were put to death for pursuing their religion. We may therefore conclude from Tacitus that Christianity spread far and fast and that being a Christian could be very difficult. The time span between the beginnings of Christianity and the Great Fire in Rome was considerably under forty years.

The rapid spread of Christianity may have relevance for investigating the reliability of the Gospels. Surely, the more widespread Christianity became, the harder it would have been for anyone to change its message and beliefs. This would have been particularly so if the Christians were paying a high price for their faith. Scholars who argue that core Christian beliefs, such as the idea that Jesus rose from the dead after his crucifixion, were innovations arising as Christianity spread by word of mouth need to suggest *when* this might have happened. The idea that core beliefs arose decades after Christianity began to spread does not explain why Christianity proved popular in the first place or how people who adhered to a version of Christianity without these beliefs later came to adopt them.

The later agreement of Christians that Jesus Christ was God's Son, prophesied by the Jewish Scriptures, crucified for sins, and raised from the dead by God is best explained by supposing that these and other central beliefs were established *before* Christianity began to spread.

Pliny the Younger

We come now to our second Roman witness, Pliny the Younger (born AD 61/62; died after AD 111). Toward the end of a distinguished career, during which he held many public offices, Pliny became governor of Bithynia and Pontus, a region in northwest Turkey. He governed there around 109–111.[7] He wrote specifically to the emperor Trajan (ruled 98–117) on a number of occasions. Pliny's most famous letter is the one he wrote to Trajan asking for advice on how to deal with Christians (*Epistles* 10.96). He wrote:

> It is my rule, sir, to refer to you all matters of which I am unsure. For who is more capable of guiding my uncertainty or informing my ignorance? Having never been present at any trials of the Christians, I am unacquainted with the method and limits to be observed either in examining or punishing them. I have also been in great doubt whether any difference is to be made on account of age, or any distinction allowed between the youngest and the adult; whether recanting allows a pardon, or whether if a man has been once a Christian it does not help him to recant; whether the mere profession of Christianity, albeit without crimes, or only the crimes associated with it are punishable.
>
> In the meanwhile, the method I have observed towards those who have been denounced to me as Christians is this: I interrogated them whether they were Christians. If they

---

7. Or perhaps AD 111–13.

confessed it I repeated the question a second and a third time, adding the threat of capital punishment. If they still persevered, I ordered them to be led off to execution. For whatever the nature of their belief might be, I could at least feel no doubt that stubbornness and inflexible obstinacy deserved punishment. There were others also possessed with the same madness, but being citizens of Rome I directed them to be sent there.

These accusations spread (as is usually the case) from the mere fact of the matter being investigated and several forms of the mischief came to light. A placard was put up, without any signature, accusing a large number of persons by name. Those who denied that they were, or ever had been, Christians, who repeated after me an invocation to the gods, and offered adoration, with wine and incense, to your statue, which I had ordered to be brought for this purpose, together with the images of the gods, and who finally cursed Christ—all things it is said that no real Christian can be forced to do—I thought they should be discharged. Others who were named by that informer at first confessed themselves Christians, but soon after denied it, saying that they had been, but they had ceased, some three years ago, others many years ago, and a few as much as twenty years ago. They all worshipped your statue and the images of the gods, and cursed Christ.

They affirmed, however, the whole of their guilt or error was that they were in the habit of meeting on a certain fixed day before it was light, and of singing in alternate verses a hymn to Christ as to a god, and of binding themselves by a solemn oath, not to wicked deeds, but never to commit any fraud, theft, or adultery, never to falsify their word, nor to deny a pledge when they were called upon to deliver it up. After this it was their custom to separate, and then reassemble to partake of food—but food of an ordinary and innocent kind. Even this practice, however, they had abandoned after the publication of my edict, by which, according to your orders, I had forbidden political associations. I therefore thought it the more necessary to extract the real truth, with the assistance of torture, from two female slaves, who were called deaconesses: but I could discover nothing more than depraved and excessive superstition.

I have therefore adjourned the proceedings and hastened to consult you. For the matter seemed to me well worth referring to you—especially considering the numbers endangered. Many persons of all ages and ranks and of both sexes are being and will be called to trial. For this contagious superstition is not confined only to the cities, but has also spread through the villages and rural districts. It seems possible, however, to check and correct this. It is certain at least that the temples, which had almost become deserted, are now beginning to be visited again; and the sacred rites, after a long interlude, are again being revived. There is a general demand for sacrificial animals, for which up to now only rarely were purchasers found. From this it is easy to imagine that a multitude of people may be reclaimed from this error, if a door is left open for them to change their minds.[8]

Trajan then replied more briefly to Pliny (whom he called Secundus; *Epistles* 10.97):

The method you have pursued, my Secundus, in sifting the cases of those denounced to you as Christians is proper. It is not possible to lay down any general rule which can be applied as the fixed standard in all cases of

---

8. My translation is freely adapted from William Melmoth, *Pliny, Letters*, rev. W. M. L. Hutchinson, vol. 2 (London: William Heinemann, 1924), 401–5.

this nature. No search should be made for these people. When they are denounced and found guilty they must be punished; with the restriction, however, that when an individual denies that he is a Christian, and gives proof of it, i.e. by adoring our gods, he shall be pardoned on the ground of repentance, even though he may have formerly incurred suspicion. Anonymous accusations must not be admitted in evidence against anyone, as it is introducing a very dangerous precedent, and by no means agreeable to our times.[9]

Large Numbers of Christians

We can draw several conclusions from this correspondence. One is that neither Pliny nor Emperor Trajan liked Christians. Another is that it was often difficult to be a Christian. A third is that there appear to have been large numbers of Christians in Pliny's area, a theme found also in Tacitus's *Annals*. Tacitus spoke of a "vast number" in Rome, and here the governor of Bithynia is writing to the emperor saying that so many people in his area had become Christians that temples were becoming nearly deserted, and sellers of sacrificial meat actually struggled to find purchasers. Of course, we can detect rhetorical flourish behind Pliny's depictions of deserted temples and rare purchasers of sacrificial meat. But despite this, he was writing to the emperor and certainly would not have wanted to risk giving Trajan the impression that he was reporting untruthfully on his province.

The situation in this non-Christian source is strikingly similar to one described in the book of Acts in the New Testament, which is relevant to the question of Gospel reliability, since the style of the book of Acts indicates that it was written

---

9. My translation is freely adapted from Melmoth, *Pliny, Letters*, 2:407.

by the same person who wrote Luke's Gospel. Acts 19 describes the situation further south in Ephesus, where a huge riot arose because so many people were turning to Christianity that the silversmiths were not able to sell their images of the gods.

The most natural reading of these sources together is that very large numbers of people were becoming Christians. The mere existence of many Christians does not for one moment have to mean that their beliefs were true. False belief can spread fast. The numbers do, however, make some explanations of early Christianity more difficult.

Those who might say that Christian belief arose by a gradual evolution usually maintain that some of the core beliefs arose only after a long time. But if core ideas, such as that Jesus Christ died as a sacrifice for sins and then rose again bodily, are only late additions to Christian belief, how do we explain the wide geographical distribution of Christians with these beliefs? Many independent early Christian sources contain these beliefs explicitly or implicitly. It is not really possible to account for the later uniformity in Christian belief on these matters if the vast numbers of earlier Christians did not also believe them. Nor can one suppose that in those days, when it was difficult and even dangerous to travel, it would have been possible for any group without political authority to *impose* a major change of beliefs on so large and widespread a set of adherents.

Just One God

A further feature of the correspondence is worth dwelling upon. Pliny and Emperor Trajan agreed on the test to be applied to suspected Christians: suspects had to show that they were not Christian by worshiping the Roman gods. The emperor demonstrated an awareness of what Christians stood for when he wrote, "When an individual denies that he is a Christian, and gives proof of it, i.e. by adoring our gods . . ." Trajan knew enough about Christian belief to be satisfied that this was an adequate test.

Pliny himself had several tests. Other than cursing Christ, all the other tests revolved round worshiping the Roman gods (among whom the emperor was, in some ways, included). None of this is surprising, given what we know of later Christian belief in one sole God. This belief is reflected consistently in the earliest surviving Christian documents.[10] Nor is it hard to find where this came from since everyone agrees that Christianity arose from within Judaism, which had a strong belief that there was only one God and that he alone should be worshiped. The simplest view of the evidence is that Christians *maintained* the earlier belief of the Jews that there was just one God, the Creator, who was absolutely distinct from everything he had created.

However, this is where Pliny's letter to Trajan surprises us, because it reports an early Christian meeting, as described by those who had renounced Christianity three years, "many" years, or even as much as twenty years previously. Go back roughly twenty years from about the year AD 111, and we see that the governor of Bithynia was giving the emperor a description of *a first-century Christian meeting*.

Apart from the recurring emphasis on integrity in business and family and on general honesty, we also see that early Christians are depicted as assembling before dawn and *singing to Christ* "as to a god" in a way that it is hard to view as anything other than worship. There is no mention of singing to God; rather Christ is the focus of the early Christian

---

10. E.g., 1 Corinthians 8:6; Ephesians 4:6; 1 Timothy 2:5.

service. Since there is no indefinite article in Latin, Pliny's phrase *quasi deo* could mean "as if to God" or "as if to a god." But we have just seen that, according to the emperor, the foolproof test of whether someone was a Christian was whether he or she was prepared to worship Roman gods. Christians were *not* prepared to do so precisely because they retained the Jewish rejection of worship of any being except the Creator God.

How then could they worship Christ? The answer is as simple as it is mathematical.

In popular ideas of how Christianity arose, it is often suggested that worshiping Christ and treating him as God must have arisen through a gradual developmental process. A problem with this is that the Jewish monotheism from which Christianity arose maintained a sharp dichotomy between the one Creator and everything he created. There was a strict cap on the number of gods at just one. That means that those adhering to Jewish categories would not have imagined Christ as a demigod somewhere in a transition from merely human to fully divine. In Judaism there were no half gods, and so Christ would never have been considered halfway from human to divine, resulting in the impossible number of one and a half gods. In classic Jewish categories, there simply was no evolutionary path of gradually assigning more and more honor to a being until it was viewed as God.[11]

Besides, even *after* Trajan heard of how the early Christians sang worship to Christ, he still maintained that mere worship

---

11. Rabbinic expert Daniel Boyarin claims that "many Israelites at the time of Jesus were expecting a Messiah who would be divine and come to earth in the form of a human." This position is controversial but still maintains that belief in Jesus's divinity was early. Boyarin says, "The idea of Jesus as divine-human Messiah goes back to the very beginning of the Christian movement, to Jesus himself, and even before that." See Boyarin, *The Jewish Gospels: The Story of the Jewish Christ* (New York: New Press, 2012), 6, 7.

of the Roman gods was enough evidence that someone was no longer a Christian. So, as far as the emperor understood Christianity, he presumed that Christ was effectively the deity of the early Christians.

In summary, the picture we get from Tacitus and Pliny agrees in important ways with what we find within the New Testament. We can conclude that Christ was executed under Pontius Pilate and was shortly afterward treated as God by a group of people who retained the core Jewish belief in one God. Christianity also spread rapidly, and it was at times difficult to be a Christian.

All of this raises the question of why Christianity spread so quickly and how someone who had been publicly executed by the Romans, and thus shown to be a loser, could so soon be viewed as one to be worshiped. Jews were averse to worshiping mere humans, and though some non-Jews (Gentiles) admired the Jews, many did not. The spread of a religion that would have looked so Jewish among large numbers of non-Jews in the Roman Empire requires a convincing explanation.

Flavius Josephus

Our third non-Christian writer is the Jewish historian Flavius Josephus. He was born around the year AD 37 or 38 and died some time after AD 100. Josephus was commander of the Jewish forces in Galilee during their initial rebellion against Rome in AD 66. He was captured by the Romans in 67 and claims to have predicted that Vespasian would become emperor in July 69. Josephus found favor with Vespasian and subsequent emperors, became a citizen of Rome, and took the name Flavius in accordance with Vespasian's family's name. During his later life in Rome, he wrote the works shown in table 1.2.

Table 1.2. Writings of Josephus

Short Title	Content	Length	Approximate Date
Jewish War	On the Jewish conflict with Rome, AD 66–73	7 books	AD 79
Jewish Antiquities	A history of the Jews, beginning with creation	20 books	AD 93
Life of Josephus	An autobiography focused on the Jewish conflict with Rome	1 book	AD 93
Against Apion	A defense of Judaism stressing its antiquity	2 books	AD 95

Josephus is the single most important historian for events in first-century Palestine, and is of particular interest since his history *Jewish Antiquities* speaks about Jesus Christ and also John the Baptist,[12] a major figure in the Gospels.

The Greek manuscripts of Josephus's *Jewish Antiquities* mention Jesus Christ in two places, of which one is judged by many scholars to be a secondary addition (i.e., not by Josephus) or to have suffered contamination during textual copying.[13] The other passage tells of how the Jewish high priest Ananus, making the most of a power vacuum while there was no governor in AD 62, acted as follows: "[Ananus] convened the judges of the Sanhedrin and brought before them a man named James, the brother of Jesus who was called the Christ, and certain others. He accused them of having transgressed the law and delivered them up to be stoned."[14] At the time of this report Josephus was an adult, and this event took place in his own city of Jerusalem, where he was probably then living. It confirms the statements in Matthew 13:55 and Mark 6:3 that Jesus had a brother called

---

12. Josephus, *Antiquities* 18.116–19. See also the discussion under the heading "Two Wives," beginning on p. 94.

13. Josephus, *Antiquities* 18.63–64.

14. Josephus, *Antiquities* 20.200, Loeb Classical Library 456 (Cambridge, MA: Harvard University Press, 1965), 107–9.

James.[15] According to first-century Christians, James was the leader of the Christians in Jerusalem (Acts 15:13; Galatians 1:19; 2:9). So it seems that the high priest Ananus was engaging in religious persecution of James and other Christians, perceiving them to be violators of the Jewish law.

The portrait of this situation given by Josephus fits well with what we have already seen from Tacitus and Pliny, as well as with the frequent accounts of persecution within the New Testament. The non-Christian sources basically agree with the Christian ones in recording the difficulties early Christians experienced.

However, the reference in Josephus is also rather different from references in Tacitus and Pliny. Those two classical writers give evidence for how far and how fast Christianity spread. Josephus, however, lets us see that even after Christianity had been going for several decades, there were still family members involved in the movement of Jesus's followers. This is interesting because, to have such a role, James would have had to believe, or at least pretend to believe, that his crucified brother was the promised Jewish deliverer, the Messiah, since that is what the name *Christ* means. Moreover, James's death for his faith makes it far more natural to assume his sincerity and that he genuinely believed his brother to be the Messiah.

Certain things follow from this. A brother, even a younger brother, is usually knowledgeable about the lives of other members of his family. For instance, James would most likely have grown up hearing about where his brother Jesus was born, something of his ancestry, and whether his parents presented Joseph as the biological father to Jesus. If James was both a family member and sincere in believing his brother to be the Messiah, his leadership of the church in Jerusalem would probably *not*

---

15. "Brother" could mean "half-brother," and in Matthew 13:55 the use of this title is presented as compatible with the view in Matthew 1:18–25 that neither Joseph nor any other man had contributed to Mary's pregnancy.

have provided an environment in which major new teachings were easily accepted.

Matthew and Luke, which are normally dated to the first century, testify to the belief that Jesus was born of a virgin in Bethlehem, the town the Old Testament prophet Micah had said would be the place from which the future ruler of Israel would arise (Micah 5:2). All four Gospels attest to the belief that Jesus was descended from David.[16] Skeptical readers of the New Testament might naturally assume that these beliefs arose through exaggerations over time as word of Jesus as Messiah spread. The problem with this is finding a context in which such embellishments *could* spread.

It is actually most natural to assume that in the first thirty or so years of Christianity, more than one sincere member of the family of Jesus held a key role in the early church. According to 1 Corinthians 9:5 (written ca. AD 56) not just one brother, but "the brothers" of Jesus traveled with their wives, spreading the Christian message. This suggests a situation in which the sprouting of novel beliefs about the family origins of Jesus would have been hard.

But is it then likely that such beliefs arose after AD 62, when James had died? The problem with supposing that novel beliefs arose later is that, by then, Christianity had spread so far and so fast that it would have been difficult to introduce innovations. For a start, anyone wanting to spread a new doctrine would have had to travel widely to advance the belief, and would also have had to overcome resistance as he sought to displace the established belief.

16. In John 7:42, the belief that Jesus was born in Bethlehem and descended from David is conveyed using irony. For possible material evidence that some people at the time of the New Testament claimed that they could trace their genealogy back to David, see *Corpus Inscriptionum Iudaeae/Palaestinae*, vol. 1, *Jerusalem, Part 1: 1–704*, ed. Hannah M. Cotton, Leah Di Segni, Werner Eck, Benjamin Isaac, Alla Kushnir-Stein, Haggai Misgav, Jonathan Price, Israel Roll, and Ada Yardeni (Berlin: De Gruyter, 2010), 88–90.

Take, for instance, the idea that Jesus was born in Bethlehem. If we ignore for the moment the remarkable nature of the claims that an individual who was descended from the founder of Israel's great royal dynasty was born of a virgin in the town from which a prophet had predicted a future ruler would arise, the most straightforward view of the documentary evidence would be that these beliefs were in place from when Christianity first started spreading. If a non-miraculous but otherwise similar set of beliefs was attested in documents as close to the events as were the Gospels and among people as widespread as were early Christians, few people would have any difficulty in believing these facts to be true. This would especially be the case if sincere family members were around for the opening decades of the spread of the message.

We will deal in chapter 8 with the question of the miraculous, which is a problem for some people in taking the Gospel accounts as historical. All I want to establish at this stage is that, were it not for the amazing nature of the claims made about Jesus, few would have any problem believing biographical details recorded so close to the alleged events.

We have now looked at three non-Christian writers and what they said about Jesus Christ or Christians. We have seen

- the confirmation of basic facts from the New Testament, such as Christ's death under Pontius Pilate in Judaea between AD 26 and AD 36,
- that Christ was worshiped as God early on,
- that Christ's followers often experienced persecution,
- that Christians spread far and fast,
- that some early Christian leaders would have known of Christ's family origins.

2

What Are the Four Gospels?

In the previous chapter we considered some basic information about Christianity from non-Christian sources: it began with a man called Jesus Christ in Judaea, who was executed by the Romans some time between AD 26 and AD 36. After his death his followers spread and, within decades, could be found in different parts of the Roman Empire. The same story is also told in Christian texts.

To get further into our investigation, we need to consider those Christian sources. It might be tempting to dismiss them as biased, but, as mentioned earlier, the mere fact that a writer wants to prove something does not make the writer unreliable. In what follows, the names *Matthew*, *Mark*, *Luke*, and *John* refer to the Gospels, not their alleged authors, unless the context makes it obvious that I am talking about a person.

It is widely agreed that the four Gospels are the earliest extended accounts of Jesus's life and teaching. Some scholars have claimed that the *Gospel of Thomas*, which was certainly not written by Jesus's disciple Thomas, should also be accepted as an important independent early source about Jesus, but it is probably dependent on the New Testament writings.[1] Bart Ehrman, widely known as an ex-Christian and a skeptic of Christianity, puts it this way:

> As we will see in a moment, the oldest and best sources we have for knowing about the life of Jesus . . . are the four Gospels of the New Testament, Matthew, Mark, Luke, and John. This is not simply the view of Christian historians who have a high opinion of the New Testament and its historical worth; it is the view of all serious historians of antiquity of every kind, from committed evangelical Christians to hardcore atheists.[2]

The four Gospels were not chosen as a result of political power, but rather they became accepted by early Christians as the best sources for information about Jesus's life without any central authority pressuring others to accept them. Already by the late second century and early third century, the four Gospels were a recognized group, as we see from the following facts.

The Chester Beatty Library in Dublin houses a manuscript called Papyrus 45, which contains the four Gospels and the book of Acts. This manuscript was produced in southern Egypt, probably in the first half of the third century.[3]

---

1. For evidence of the dependence of the *Gospel of Thomas* on New Testament writings, see S. J. Gathercole, *The Composition of the Gospel of Thomas: Original Language and Influences* (Cambridge: Cambridge University Press, 2012).

2. Bart D. Ehrman, *Truth and Fiction in* The Da Vinci Code (Oxford: Oxford University Press, 2004), 102.

3. Dublin, Chester Beatty Library, Papyrus Chester Beatty I. There is also one leaf of Papyrus 45 in Vienna: Austrian National Library, Papyrus Greek 31974. From a similar date comes the incomplete Vatican manuscript Papyrus 75 or Papyrus Bodmer XIV–XV, which contains Luke followed by John. Manuscript dates are generally based mainly on handwriting and the archaeological context in which a manuscript was found. Scholars date handwritings in biblical manuscripts partly by comparing them with the handwriting in legal documents, which frequently have dates written on them. The dating of

Going back a little further, we find that Irenaeus, bishop of Lyon in France, writing around the year AD 185, said that God gave the gospel in fourfold form, referring to the four Gospels.

Even earlier than this, perhaps around the year 173, a man called Tatian had made a single chronologically ordered retelling of the story of Jesus based on the four Gospels. This work, which became known as the *Diatessaron*, was most probably produced in Syria. Though it does not survive today, it is believed to have influenced many harmonies of the Gospels in the Middle Ages.

Thus, by the early third century, evidence from France, southern Egypt, and Syria all shows that the four Gospels were held to be a special collection that belonged together.[4] In other words, these four books were treated together as the best source for information about Jesus long before any central city, group, or individual in Christianity possessed enough power to impose the collection on other people. It is most natural to suppose that the credentials of the four books themselves are why they were so widely accepted.

Four Is a Lot

It is rarely appreciated that for us to have four Gospels about Jesus is remarkable. That is an abundance of material to have about any individual of that period. In fact, even though Jesus was on the periphery of the Roman Empire, we have as many early sources about his life and teaching as we have about activities and conversations of Tiberius, emperor during Jesus's

---

manuscripts this way is not exact, but scholars are usually confident enough to date a manuscript to within a range of a hundred years.

4. For evidence of an early four-Gospel collection, see Charles E. Hill, *Who Chose the Gospels? Probing the Great Gospel Conspiracy* (Oxford: Oxford University Press, 2010).

public activities. The life of Tiberius (reigned AD 14–37) and the life of Jesus are recorded in four main sources each, as shown in tables 2.1 and 2.2.[5]

Table 2.1. Main sources about Emperor Tiberius

Author and Work	Words	Earliest Copy	Date Written	Language
Velleius Paterculus, *Roman History* 2.94–131	6,489	16th century	AD 30	Latin
Tacitus, *Annals* 1–6	48,200	9th century	after AD 110*	Latin
Suetonius, *Tiberius*	9,310	9th century	after AD 120	Latin
Cassius Dio, *Roman History* 57–58	14,293	9th century	after AD 200	Greek

* I have used an earlier date here for the *Annals* than in table 1.1 (p. 18) since our table here is of minimal dates, not of probable dates. It is also possible that Tacitus was working on the early books of the *Annals* considerably before the final publication.

Table 2.2. Main sources about Jesus*

Gospel	Words	Earliest Complete Copy	Earliest Incomplete Copy	Language
Matthew	18,347	4th century	2nd/3rd century	Greek
Mark	11,103	4th century	3rd century	Greek
Luke	19,463	4th century	3rd century	Greek
John	15,445	4th century	2nd century	Greek

* Word statistics are based on *The Greek New Testament, Produced at Tyndale House, Cambridge* (Wheaton, IL: Crossway; Cambridge: Cambridge University Press, 2017), omitting Mark 16:9–20.

Apart from Velleius Paterculus, who was contemporary with Tiberius, all the sources about Tiberius came eighty or

5. All figures are approximate, and allowance should be made for textual uncertainty and the imprecision involved in automated word counts. The figures were generated from online electronic texts accessed March 14, 2018: for Velleius Paterculus, http://penelope.uchicago.edu/Thayer/E/home.html; for Tacitus and Suetonius, http://www.perseus.tufts.edu; for Cassius Dio, http://remacle.org/bloodwolf/historiens/. The figure for Tacitus would be higher, but for the fact that most of *Annals* book 5 does not survive.

more years after the events they narrate. The earliest copies came much later, and the works have far less manuscript attestation than do the Gospels. As we will see below, almost certainly the Gospels are much closer to the activities of Jesus than eighty years.

In two particular areas the records about Tiberius might seem superior. The first is that Velleius Paterculus wrote as a contemporary. However, Paterculus was a propagandist for Tiberius, composing flattery, perhaps under the patronage of Tiberius. For this reason, his testimony is usually valued less than that of the three later writers. By contrast, the Gospel writers were certainly not under political pressure from a superior to write what they did. If Tacitus and Suetonius are to be believed, Tiberius was responsible for the execution of many individuals suspected of writing against him. Of course, Paterculus tells us nothing about that.

The second advantage for the records about Tiberius is the length of the six books of Tacitus's *Annals* that deal with the reign of Tiberius. These appear much longer than the Gospels. However, though these six books all deal with the *period* of Tiberius's reign, they are not all *about* Tiberius but, rather, focus on the many events and intrigues that happened while he was emperor.[6] Likewise, not all of the text from Cassius Dio is about Tiberius. By contrast, apart from short parts of Matthew and Luke that appear to focus on John the Baptist but actually highlight Jesus, all four Gospels are exclusively focused on Jesus. It may thus be concluded that Jesus has more extended text about him, in generally closer proximity to his life, than his contemporary Tiberius, the most famous person in the then-known world.

---

6. Likewise the chapters in Velleius Paterculus are not all about Tiberius (e.g., *Roman History* 2.117–19).

Of course, both Tiberius and Jesus have other records about them, which give us less historical information than the extended biographies. For Tiberius, these include coins and numerous sporadic references in historians. For Jesus, these include all the other books of the New Testament.

However, this comparison between the records for Tiberius and for Jesus should not be pushed too far. On its own, it does not provide reason to suppose that the Gospel records are necessarily superior to those about Tiberius. The comparison, rather, provides this perspective: the amount of text we have about Jesus is good relative to one of the best-known figures from antiquity.

Overview of the Gospels

At least by the time of Irenaeus (writing ca. AD 185), the authors of the four Gospels are identified as the following:[7]

- Matthew, a tax collector from Capernaum (Matthew 9:9; 10:3), was one of Jesus's twelve disciples, also called apostles.
- Mark, not one of the Twelve, was the apostle Peter's interpreter in Rome. Generally identified as John Mark, whose mother, Mary, had a property in Jerusalem (Acts 12:12), he was a cousin of Barnabas (Colossians 4:10), who originated from Cyprus (Acts 4:36).
- Luke, not one of the Twelve, was a medical doctor (Colossians 4:14) who accompanied Paul on some of his travels round the Mediterranean and was the only New Testament writer who may have been a Gentile.
- John son of Zebedee, was one of the Twelve, the younger brother of James, and a fisherman from Capernaum.

---

7. Irenaeus, *Against Heresies* 3.11.8. See also the early second-century writer Papias, quoted in Eusebius, *Ecclesiastical History* 3.39.

We will consider later some evidence supporting these attributions, but at this stage we note that only Matthew and John are said to have been eyewitnesses to Jesus. Mark might have been an eyewitness to some events, but the early second-century writer Papias says he got his information from Peter, who in some ways was the leader of the twelve disciples.[8] Luke's Gospel implies that the author was not an eyewitness, but states that the author carefully checked all the facts with eyewitnesses. Since neither Mark nor Luke was an eyewitness, it is hard to see a motive for anyone to attach their names to the Gospels unless they were the real authors.[9]

The Gospels are not like modern biographies, which might give equal attention to each period of the subject's life. The Gospels focus disproportionately on the events of the week up to and including the crucifixion of Jesus and his resurrection. Only Matthew and Luke specifically record Jesus's birth, and only Luke gives us an account of an event between his birth and his adult career.

When we look at the Gospels they appear to be grouped as three plus one. Matthew, Mark, and Luke are more similar to each other than they are to John. In language, themes, phraseology, and order Matthew, Mark, and Luke have so much in common that nowadays they are called the Synoptic Gospels, from the sense that they see events with the same optic or vision. That said, each of the Synoptic Gospels has its own special relationship with material in John's Gospel too. But the difference between the Synoptic Gospels and John is pronounced. The Synoptics report Jesus telling stories known as parables. John does not. John reports that Jesus made a series of claims about

---

8. Eusebius, *Ecclesiastical History* 3.39.
9. For a defense of the traditional authorship of the Gospels, see Brant Pitre, *The Case for Jesus: The Biblical and Historical Evidence for Christ* (New York: Image, 2016), 12–54.

himself, seven in particular, beginning with "I am the . . . ," such as "I am the bread of life" (John 6:35), "I am the door" (John 10:9), and "I am the way, the truth, and the life" (John 14:6). The Synoptic Gospels have none of these. These are just a few examples of a great many differences.

Contrast that with the relationships among the Synoptic Gospels. In one instance Matthew and Luke both record speech attributed to John the Baptist using nearly identical wording. During a sequence of forty-one words in Greek there are only three small differences.

> But when he saw many of the Pharisees and Sadducees coming to his baptism, he said to them, "You brood of vipers! Who warned you to flee from the wrath to come? Bear *fruit in keeping with* repentance. And do not *presume* to say to yourselves, 'We have Abraham as our father,' for I tell you, God is able from these stones to raise up children for Abraham." (Matthew 3:7–9)

> He said therefore to the crowds that came out to be baptized by him, "You brood of vipers! Who warned you to flee from the wrath to come? Bear *fruits in keeping with* repentance. And do not *begin* to say to yourselves, 'We have Abraham as our father,' for I tell you, God is able from these stones to raise up children for Abraham." (Luke 3:7–8)[10]

We see immediately that the wording introducing John the Baptist's speech is different in the two Gospels. But in the speech itself, only three words differ in the Greek. "Fruit" is singular in Matthew and plural in Luke. That means that the Greek adjective translated "in keeping with" has to match the noun in each Gospel, a small difference not seen in the English translation. Finally, Matthew has "presume" where Luke has "begin."

---

10. I have adjusted a punctuation mark and subsequent capitalization in one place.

This closeness of wording, along with many similar examples, leads scholars to conclude that one of the Gospels used the other as a source, or that there was a common source behind both.

People have often sought to map out the relationships among the Synoptic Gospels statistically, speaking about percentages of similarity or difference between them. This is useful, but we must remember that percentages of similarity will vary depending on how we count. If the same word is used in two Gospels but in different grammatical forms or in slightly different positions in sentences, the uses could be counted as a similarity or a difference, depending on what was being measured. We should therefore not be surprised that numbers differ.

If we take the strictest way of counting and consider only words that are identical in grammatical form, we still find substantial correlations between Matthew, Mark, and Luke in passages where two or three of them have parallels (see table 2.3).[11]

Table 2.3. Correlations among the Gospels

Gospels	Exact Word Forms in Common
Matthew, Mark, and Luke	1,852
Only Matthew and Mark	2,735
Only Matthew and Luke	2,386
Only Mark and Luke	1,165

The earliest belief about the order of the writing of the Gospels seems to be that Matthew was written first, followed by Mark, Luke, and John, in that order.[12] But for over a century now, a majority of scholars have held that Mark came first.

11. These data are taken from Andris Abakuks, "A Statistical Study of the Triple-Link Model in the Synoptic Problem," *Journal of the Royal Statistical Society: Series A* 169, pt. 1 (2006): 49–60.
12. Eusebius, *Ecclesiastical History* 6.25, citing Origen (ca. AD 185–254).

The most common scholarly explanation for the similarities between the Gospels has been that Mark was used by both Matthew and Luke. Since the common material between Matthew and Luke consists mainly of *sayings*, scholars supposed that they might have copied from a separate source of sayings. As the German word for "source" is *Quelle*, scholars call this hypothetical source Q.[13] A smaller but influential group of scholars claim that Q was unnecessary. There is no ancient record of it, and we can adequately explain the similarities between Matthew and Luke by a direct connection between them.[14] Though Q could be used just as a neutral label designating material common to Matthew and Luke, but not in Mark, it tends to be used to refer to the idea of a specific *unified written* source. We can call this the Q Hypothesis, which is often called the Two Source Hypothesis, because Mark and Q are claimed to be two major sources of Matthew and Luke. Some people elaborate this to talk of a Four Source Hypothesis, because there are also things unique to Matthew and unique to Luke, suggesting that they come from sources we could call *M* and *L*, after Matthew and Luke.

A couple of things flow from these discussions: (1) We can categorize different types of material in Matthew, Mark, and Luke by how much they overlap with each other. Since we can speak of different kinds of material, any explanation of the Gospels needs to be compatible with the patterns of interrelationships the texts display. (2) Scholars who have believed that Matthew and Luke used Mark often do not treat Matthew and Luke as independent sources where they overlap with Mark.

---

13. This view is argued for in John S. Kloppenborg, *Q, the Earliest Gospel: An Introduction to the Original Stories and Sayings of Jesus* (Louisville: Westminster John Knox, 2008).

14. One of the ablest proponents of this view is Mark Goodacre in various writings, including *The Case against Q: Studies in Markan Priority and the Synoptic Problem* (Harrisburg, PA: Trinity Press International, 2002).

I will not take a position here on the order in which the Gospels were written, nor on the exact relationship between them. I want to argue that the case for the historical reliability of the Gospels can work with various views about the relationships between the Gospels. I will, however, seek to make the case that information throughout the Gospels can be shown to be reliable, whether the material overlaps with what is in other Gospels or not.

The five main categories of material we will find are in (1) Matthew only; (2) Luke only; (3) Mark (though possibly also in Matthew and/or Luke); (4) Matthew and Luke, but not Mark (i.e., Q); and (5) John only. There are also many cases where Matthew, Mark, and Luke (if you prefer, Mark and Q) overlap. So whether we think of the four Gospels as four independent witnesses or as five different sorts of material, the chief result is that we have multiple witnesses to things. Even if one wants to argue that Luke copied ideas from Matthew or that John used Mark (though there is little *firm* evidence of that), we find an overall pattern that makes the compelling argument that the material was not all made up. Again and again we will find that supposing the authors handed on faithfully what they knew yields simple explanations, whereas supposing they made things up produces complex ones.

When Were the Gospels Written?

The Gospels do not come with particular dates written on them, though some Christian traditions do give them specific dates—all (except for some traditions about the Gospel of John) dating the Gospels before the destruction of Jerusalem in AD 70.[15]

---

15. For instance, the manuscript Codex Cyprius (also known as K or 017, from the ninth or tenth century, Bibliothèque nationale de France Greek manuscript 63) dates Matthew, Mark, and Luke as eight, ten, and fifteen years after the ascension of Christ into heaven, which is dated forty days after the resurrection on the basis of Acts 1:3.

Table 2.4 shows date ranges proposed by some non-Christian scholars: (1) by some Jewish scholars, (2) by a Jewish historian, Shaye Cohen,[16] and (3) by a prominent agnostic scholar, Bart Ehrman.[17]

Table 2.4. Proposed dates of Gospel composition

	The Jewish Annotated New Testament*	Cohen	Ehrman
Matthew	80–90	80s	80–85
Mark	64–72	ca. 70	65–70
Luke	"toward the end of the first century"	80s	80–85
John	70–130	ca. 90–100	95

* Amy-Jill Levine and Marc Zvi Brettler, eds., *The Jewish Annotated New Testament*, 2nd ed., New Revised Standard Version Bible Translation (Oxford: Oxford University Press, 2017), 9, 67, 107, 168–69.

These dates are fairly typical among scholars, but we should notice that if the traditional view of authorship of the Gospels is correct, Matthew and John were written by people already active as disciples of Jesus no later than AD 33,[18] Mark was by someone who was able to be an assistant to Barnabas and Paul no later than about 50,[19] and Luke was by someone who accompanied Paul in the 50s and early 60s on journeys to Turkey, Greece, Judaea, and Rome.[20] Arguments for the tradi-

16. Shaye J. D. Cohen, *From the Maccabees to the Mishnah*, 3rd ed. (Louisville: Westminster John Knox, 2014), 16–17.

17. Bart D. Ehrman, *The New Testament: A Historical Introduction to the Early Christian Writings* (Oxford: Oxford University Press, 1997), 41. I give, in the table, the dates from the figure on p. 41, but on p. 40 Ehrman indicates that these are not to be understood with great precision, and he distances himself slightly from these dates: "In addition, most historians think that Mark was the first of our Gospels to be written, sometime between the mid 60s to early 70s. Matthew and Luke were probably produced some ten or fifteen years later, perhaps around 80 or 85. John was written perhaps ten years after that, in 90 or 95."

18. The latest likely date for the crucifixion. See chap. 8, n. 34.

19. Mark's appearance in Acts 12:25 had to occur considerably before Acts 18:12, when Gallio was proconsul of Achaea, around AD 51–52.

20. Luke and Acts have the same style and are widely agreed to have come from the same author. The author of Acts refers to himself and his traveling companions as

tional authors are therefore likely to provide indirect support for significantly earlier dates, unless one is inclined to suppose that the authors wrote toward the ends of unusually long lives, especially when life expectancy was shorter than now.

The sorts of dates given by the scholars above are often based in part on Gospel references, from the lips of Jesus, to the destruction of Jerusalem or the temple in AD 70. But if we allow that Jesus could predict future events, a major objection to earlier dates is removed.

Most forms of modern Judaism or agnosticism are belief systems that, by definition, deny the Gospels' presentation of Jesus as the long-prophesied, miracle-performing Son of God, who was ultimately raised from the dead. However, the dates given above show that mainstream scholars who disbelieve that Jesus was the Messiah nevertheless date the Gospels within the time limits of reliable memory. If one is open to the possibility that the portrait of Jesus's identity in the Gospels is actually true, there are few strong reasons why the Gospels could not be considerably earlier.

I prefer earlier dates over all those given above, but this book is not going to argue for particular dates for the Gospels. Rather, it will propose that the Gospels are best seen as coming from the first generation of Christians and that this fits well with traditional views of their authorship.

"we" on various occasions between Acts 16:10 and 28:16, indicating himself as a fellow traveler with Paul.

3

Did the Gospel Authors
Know Their Stuff?

One test of the Gospels' veracity is whether they display familiarity with the time and places they wrote about. If they do not, that quickly reveals that they cannot be trusted historically. If they do, that does not on its own demonstrate that all of what they wrote is true. It merely shows that the writers had enough know-how to write true stories, and it eliminates the objection that they were too distant from events to be trusted.

Although we live in an age when we have easy access to advance information about anywhere we go, we still tend to be surprised by aspects of geography and culture whenever we travel. Now imagine if someone asked you to write a story about events in a distant place you had never visited, and you were not allowed to use the Internet for research. Even with the wonderful libraries we have today, you would struggle to get all the information together to write a detailed story that fitted what a local person would know. This is because of the many aspects of your destination you would have to get right, and getting only *most* of them right would not make a story sound authentic. You would have to investigate its architecture, culture, economics, geography, language, law, politics, religion, social stratification, weather, and much more. You would even need to ensure that the characters in your tale were given names that were plausible for the historical and geographical setting of your narrative. All this requires effort and is not easily done.

In this chapter we will apply a number of tests to the Gospels to find out whether they show knowledge of these sorts of things from the time and places they describe.

The Test of Geography

The level of geographical knowledge of the Gospel writers can be seen, to some degree, in simple tables (3.1–4) of all the places they record in Israel/Palestine and its surroundings.[1]

Table 3.1. Gospel writers' references to towns

Towns	Matthew	Mark	Luke	John
Aenon				✓
Arimathea	✓	✓	✓	✓
Bethany	✓	✓	✓	✓
Bethlehem	✓		✓	✓
Bethphage	✓	✓	✓	
Bethsaida	✓	✓	✓	✓
Caesarea Philippi	✓	✓		
Cana				✓
Capernaum	✓	✓	✓	✓
Chorazin	✓		✓	
Dalmanutha		✓		

---

1. I include in these tables Egypt, Tyre, and Sidon as places in which the story of Jesus is sometimes set, but not Babylon. I have also excluded places distant in time, i.e., Sodom and Gomorrah, and towns that are included within adjectives, e.g., Gerasene (implying Gerasa) and Magdalene (implying Magdala). My use of the word *Palestine* is not connected with its use in modern geography.

Towns	Matthew	Mark	Luke	John
Emmaus			✓	
Ephraim				✓
Gennesaret	✓	✓	✓	
Jericho	✓	✓	✓	
Jerusalem (or Zion)	✓	✓	✓	✓
Magadan	✓			
Nain			✓	
Nazareth	✓	✓	✓	✓
Rama	✓			
Salim				✓
Sidon	✓	✓	✓	
Sychar				✓
Tiberias				✓
Tyre	✓	✓	✓	
Zarephath			✓	

Table 3.2. Gospel writers' references to regions

Regions	Matthew	Mark	Luke	John
Abilene			✓	
Decapolis	✓	✓		
Egypt	✓			
Galilee	✓	✓	✓	✓
Idumaea		✓		
Ituraea			✓	
Judaea	✓	✓	✓	✓
Naphtali	✓			
Samaria			✓	✓
Sidonia			✓	
Syria	✓		✓	
Trachonitis			✓	
Zebulun	✓			

Table 3.3. Gospel writers' references to bodies of water

Bodies of Water	Matthew	Mark	Luke	John
Bethesda				✓
Kidron				✓
river Jordan	✓	✓	✓	✓
Sea of Galilee	✓	✓		✓
Siloam			✓	✓

Table 3.4. Gospel writers' references to other places

Other Places*	Matthew	Mark	Luke	John
field of Blood	✓			
Gabbatha				✓
Gethsemane	✓	✓		
Golgotha / Place of the Skull	✓	✓	✓	✓
Mount of Olives	✓	✓	✓	
Sheep Gate				✓
Solomon's Colonnade				✓

* I have not included the Praetorium mentioned in Matthew, Mark, and John, as it is not clearly a proper name.

These lists, of course, do not show that the Gospels are not largely fictional. The information in the lists, however, would be extremely surprising if we were to think of the Gospel writers as having lived in other countries, such as Egypt, Italy, Greece, or Turkey, and having made up stories about Jesus. The lists show the following:

1. All writers display knowledge of a range of localities from well known, through lesser known, to obscure.
2. No Gospel writer gains all his knowledge from the other Gospels, since each contains unique information.
3. All writers show a variety of types of geographical information.

The four Gospels demonstrate familiarity with the geography of the places they write about. In total, they mention twenty-six towns:[2] sixteen each in Matthew and Luke and thirteen each in Mark and John. Among the towns listed are not only famous places—like the religious capital, Jerusalem—but also small villages, such as Bethany (all four Gospels) and Bethphage (Matthew, Mark, and Luke). In John we find numerous minor villages mentioned: Aenon, Cana, Ephraim, Salim, and Sychar.

It is worth reflecting on how such knowledge could be obtained. In principle, one might get it through personal experience, reading, or hearing. However, it does not seem that the Gospel writers could have simply obtained their information from *reading*. No known sources hold together the particular set of information they have; and, besides, we would have to suppose that they undertook a level of literary research quite unparalleled in ancient history. If these pieces of information result from *hearing*, then the reports they heard must have been fairly precise—concerned with stories not merely for their message but also for specific details. Thus, it seems that the authors received the information either from their *experience* or from *detailed hearing*.

If anyone were inserting geographical details to make the story look authentic, he would have had to be very thorough. This is not at all the behavior we would expect from four different authors writing independently. We may also look at the frequency with which locations are mentioned within the narratives (see table 3.5). These are, of course, greater than the number of individual locations named, since many places are mentioned repeatedly.

---

2. Of these towns, Rama and Zarephath come within allusions to the Old Testament and therefore do not necessarily indicate specific geographical familiarity.

Table 3.5. Frequency of geographical references

	Matthew	Mark	Luke	John
Total Greek Words*	18,347	11,103	19,463	15,445
Towns	43	33	62	39
Regions	32	16	29	25
Bodies of water	9	6	3	8
Other places	6	5	5	4
Total places	90	60	99	76
Locations mentioned per 1,000 words	4.905	5.404	5.087	4.921

* According to *The Greek New Testament, Produced at Tyndale House, Cambridge* (Wheaton, IL: Crossway; Cambridge: Cambridge University Press, 2017), excluding Mark 16:9–20.

A striking thing is that all four Gospels, despite their differences, have a similar frequency with which they mention contemporary geography. Of course, both reliable and unreliable reporting could have much higher or lower frequencies than we find here. However, it is impractical to argue that the similarity of frequency arose in the Gospels because they were *trying* to present such details with a certain frequency.[3] After all, we see variation within the types of geographical names they mention. It is a pattern more likely to reflect the fact that the Gospel writers were *not trying* to insert place names to make their stories look authentic. The even distribution of place names in the four Gospels is unlikely to be the result of each of the four writers making a deliberate effort to spread names out, but is exactly the sort of pattern that might occur through *unconscious behavior*, recording places naturally when relevant to their stories. The similar frequencies may in fact testify to a

---

3. Greek words were generally written without spaces between, and there was no distinction between uppercase and lowercase. Therefore counting words and, in particular, geographical terms would have been difficult.

shared culture or pattern of telling stories, but certainly does not result from collusion.

Bodies of Water

The four Gospels do not just know the names of towns and places. They also know about how they relate and about the topography of Palestine.

Consider the word *sea*. According to the Gospels, Jesus spent much of his time by the Sea of Galilee. *Sea* is, of course, a rather grand word for a body of water just twenty-one kilometers (thirteen miles) in length, but from the perspective of any local Galilean who had not traveled far, this was *the* sea and did not need further description.

Matthew uses the word *sea* sixteen times. Four times it does not refer to any sea in particular,[4] but the other twelve times it has some reference to the Sea of Galilee.[5] The first explicit reference is in Matthew 4:18 (first occurrence), and it is again specified as the Sea of Galilee after Jesus goes up to the cities of Tyre and Sidon on the Mediterranean coast (Matthew 15:29). Otherwise it is simply called "the sea."[6]

Mark uses *sea* nineteen times. Twice it refers to no sea in particular (Mark 9:42; 11:23). The first occurrence in Mark is expressly the Sea of Galilee (1:16). As in Matthew, it is named specifically when Jesus returns from Tyre via Sidon to the Sea of Galilee (Mark 7:31). Otherwise it is simply "the sea."[7] This is what we would expect if Mark's Gospel really were written on the basis of information supplied to Mark by the fisherman Peter, for whom this would have been *the* sea *par excellence*.

---

4. Matthew 13:47; 18:6; 21:21; 23:15.
5. Matthew 4:15 in its context seems to refer to the Sea of Galilee.
6. Matthew 4:18 (second occurrence); 8:24, 26, 27, 32; 13:1; 14:25, 26; 17:27.
7. Mark 1:16 (second occurrence); 2:13; 3:7; 4:1 (3×), 39, 41; 5:1, 13 (2×), 21; 6:47, 48, 49.

Luke is rather different. It uses the word *sea* only three times and never in reference to a particular body of water. If, as is traditionally thought, Luke came from Antioch on the Orontes, not far from the Mediterranean, he certainly would not have thought of the tiny Sea of Galilee as *the* sea. He just calls it "the lake."[8]

John, traditionally held to be a Galilean fisherman, uses the word *sea* nine times in two scenes by the Sea of Galilee in chapters 6 and 21. The first occurrence is the most specified—"the Sea of Galilee, which is the Sea of Tiberias," where the sea is also named after Tiberias, a major town on the shore (John 6:1). Subsequent references in the same chapter are just to "the sea."[9] John again speaks of "the Sea of Tiberias" when reintroducing the lake in a new context (John 21:1), then refers back to it simply as "the sea" (John 21:7). John also tells us of the seasonal stream, the Kidron, near Jerusalem, and of two pools in Jerusalem, one of which he correctly describes as having five colonnades. (While speaking of colonnades, we should note that he also knows of Solomon's Colonnade in the temple.)

The Gospels also know that Bethsaida and Capernaum are towns located by the Sea of Galilee (Matthew 4:13; Mark 6:45). Matthew and Mark know that one can go from the Sea of Galilee directly into hill country.[10] Matthew, Mark, and Luke know that there is a Judaean desert near the Jordan.[11]

Roads and Travel

All four Gospels know that traveling to Jerusalem (elevation about 750 meters, or about 2450 feet) is correctly described as

---

8. Luke 5:1, 2; 8:22, 23, 33.
9. John 6:16, 17, 18, 19, 22, 25.
10. Matthew 14:22–23; 15:29; Mark 3:13 compared with 3:7.
11. Matthew 3:1; 4:1; 11:7; Mark 1:3–4, 12; Luke 3:2–4; 4:1.

going up.[12] Mark and Luke know that leaving Jerusalem is correctly described as *going down*.[13] This is perhaps not particularly significant, as a capital city is typically portrayed as elevated in relation to other places. There are, however, a couple of occasions when we get the impression that the Gospel writers know rather particularly the topography of the land. In Luke 10:30–31 we read of Jesus telling a story that begins as follows: "A man was *going down* from Jerusalem to Jericho, and he fell among robbers, who stripped him and beat him and departed, leaving him half dead. Now by chance a priest was *going down* that road, and when he saw him he passed by on the other side." Jericho is, in fact, the lowest city on earth, over 250 meters (over 800 feet) below sea level. Going from Jerusalem to Jericho involves a descent of approximately one kilometer. *Go down* is therefore very much the right expression. The passage assumes a direct route between Jerusalem and Jericho, which of course there is.

In John 2:12 the journey from Cana of Galilee to Capernaum is described as *going down*. Similarly, in John 4 we have an account of a nobleman coming to Jesus while Jesus is in Cana, begging him to *come down* and heal his son who is in Capernaum. The verb *come down* is repeatedly used to describe the journey from Cana to Capernaum.[14] The location of Cana is disputed, but the lowest of the candidates, Khirbet Qana, is at an elevation of about 200 meters (about 700 feet), whereas Capernaum is over 200 meters *below* sea level.[15] Likewise Luke 4:31 describes travel from Nazareth (around 350 meters, or 1150 feet above sea level) to Capernaum as *going down*.

---

12. Matthew 20:17, 18; Mark 10:32, 33; Luke 2:4, 42; 18:31; 19:28; John 2:13; 5:1; 7:8, 10, 14; 11:55; 12:20.

13. Mark 3:22; Luke 2:51; 18:14.

14. John 4:47, 49, 51.

15. Elevations are taken from http://elevationmap.net, accessed March 14, 2018. Of course, ancient elevations may have been slightly different from modern ones, but not so different as to make a difference in this argument.

Rather specific knowledge is evidenced by the words attributed to Jesus in Luke 10:13–15 (and its parallel in Matthew 11:21–23):

> Woe to you, *Chorazin*! Woe to you, *Bethsaida*! For if the mighty works done in you had been done in Tyre and Sidon, they would have repented long ago, sitting in sackcloth and ashes. But it will be more bearable in the judgment for Tyre and Sidon than for you. And you, *Capernaum*, will you be exalted to heaven? You shall be brought down to Hades.

Jesus upbraids three Jewish towns or villages—Chorazin, Bethsaida, and Capernaum—contrasting the first two with the Gentile cities of Tyre and Sidon. The little-known village Chorazin is in fact *on the road to Bethsaida* and just a couple of miles north of Capernaum. As far as we know, there was not a single literary source that could have provided this information to a Gospel author.

Luke and John both show knowledge that there are two routes between Judaea and Galilee: the hilly route via Samaria and the indirect route avoiding Samaritan areas via the Jordan valley. In Luke 9:51–53 Jesus and his disciples are refused passage through Samaria when traveling southward from Galilee to Judaea. In John 4:4 Jesus takes the route northward from Judaea to Galilee through Samaria. However, Luke also describes a journey to Jerusalem via Jericho (Luke 18:35) and then through the villages of Bethphage and Bethany (Luke 19:29). John depicts Jesus as making his final approach to Jerusalem from the east via Bethany (John 12:1).

The information in Luke and John accords with the way Matthew and Mark portray Jesus's final approach to Jerusalem. He is said to go from Galilee to the Transjordan (Matthew 19:1; Mark 10:1) and to approach Jerusalem from Jericho (Matthew

20:29; Mark 10:46) and then Bethphage, which is located by the narrative as on the Mount of Olives (Matthew 21:1; Mark 11:1).[16]

Gardens

The Gospel writers often mention details that are not recorded in any other books. Two specific gardens are mentioned: one called Gethsemane, where Jesus prayed before his arrest,[17] and one near Golgotha, the place of Jesus's crucifixion.[18] As there are no other surviving contemporary records of these place names, it is unlikely that the Gospel writers had access to geographical books that would have told them about these places. But it would have been hard for them to invent these names, because their particular linguistic shapes betray knowledge of Judaea and its languages. *Golgotha* is said in the Gospels to mean "skull,"[19] which fits well with what is found in Aramaic dialects.[20] Since before the fourth century, Jesus's tomb has been thought to be within the Church of the Holy Sepulchre, where, according to Shimon Gibson, one of the leading authorities on the archaeology of that church, John's depiction of a garden by the location of the crucifixion fits well with the archaeology.[21] Gethsemane means "oil press" (i.e., press for *olives*) and is perfectly located in the narrative on the Mount of *Olives*, which is mentioned in the Gospels as well as numerous other sources. However, nowhere do the Gospel writers draw attention to the meaning of Gethsemane and how it particularly suited the location. They just knew.

---

16. Mark 11:1 says, "Bethphage and Bethany."
17. Matthew 26:36; Mark 14:32.
18. Matthew 27:33; Mark 15:22; John 19:17, 41.
19. Matthew 27:33; Mark 15:22; John 19:17.
20. The ending of the form *gulgoltha* has changed via *-owtha* to *-otha*.
21. Shimon Gibson, *The Final Days of Jesus: The Archaeological Evidence* (New York: HarperOne, 2009), 118–22, argues that this was an area of both gardens and tombs.

What Does This Mean?

My argument is not that knowledge of these geographical details demonstrates the Gospels to be true, but rather that the idea that they got the story wrong for lack of high-quality information on the location of events is false. Either the Gospel writers themselves or people they interacted with at length were able to describe the locations of Jesus's activities in detail. Reading from the works of writers theoretically available to the Gospel writers, such as Josephus, Philo, or Strabo, would not give any one of the Gospels the array of geographical knowledge it contains, and it is not plausible that the Gospel writers each plundered literary sources for information to make their stories sound authentic.

To put this more positively: the Gospels are not merely accurate in their geography when compared with other sources; they are themselves valuable geographical sources. For instance, no historian doubts the existence of the Decapolis, a group of ten or more cities characterized particularly by non-Jewish population. These are mentioned in the works of Josephus, Pliny the Elder, and Ptolemy. But according to widely accepted dates, Mark is the first to mention the Decapolis (Mark 5:20; 7:31; see also Matthew 4:25).[22]

Three conclusions naturally follow:

- The writers either were acquainted with the land themselves or accurately recorded what was reported by others who were acquainted with the land.
- The information the writers had is consistent with what we would expect if the Gospels were by their traditional authors.
- The resulting Gospels are not what we would expect from people who made up stories at a geographical distance.

---

22. See R. Steven Notley, *In the Master's Steps: The Gospels in the Land* (Jerusalem: Carta, 2014), 51–54.

Contrast with Later Gospels—Geography

Another way we may look at this geographical information is to compare it with other ancient works called *Gospels* in antiquity or by modern scholars. One of the most famous has been the *Gospel of Thomas*, which none other than the German Bible Society prints at the back of its synopsis of the four Gospels because of its various parallels with them.[23] A text made popular by Dan Brown's *Da Vinci Code* was the *Gospel of Philip*. Then there is the *Gospel of Judas*, published by *National Geographic* magazine in 2006. All these Gospels were probably written 50–150 years after the four Gospels, but we also see that they contain much less geographical information.

The *Gospel of Thomas* mentions Judaea once, but names no other location. The *Gospel of Judas* names no locations. The *Gospel of Philip* names Jerusalem (four times), Nazara (once, a legitimate alternative spelling for Nazareth), and the Jordan (once). It must be appreciated how truly unimpressive this is. Jerusalem was the famous religious capital. No special knowledge was required to have heard of it. Jordan was the main river. Nazareth became famous because of Jesus, who was often called Jesus the Nazarene or Jesus of Nazareth. Though the *Gospel of Philip* is the least unimpressive of these Gospels, none of what is found in any of these Gospels gives a sense of familiarity with the places Jesus lived in or visited.

These later Gospels do, however, provide us with an excellent control sample. They show that sometimes people wrote about Jesus without close knowledge of what he did. The fact that the four Gospels, both as a group and individually, contrast with these other Gospels illustrates the qualitative difference between these sources.

---

23. Kurt Aland, ed., *Synopsis Quattuor Evangeliorum*, 15th ed. (Stuttgart: German Bible Society, 1996).

Names of People

One of the clearest indications of the familiarity of the Gospel writers with the context they are writing about comes in the form of their knowledge of personal names.

A series of scholarly studies has shown that, though Jews were located in many places in the Roman Empire, the different locations had rather distinct naming patterns, and the popularity of various names among Jews outside Palestine bore little relationship to those inside Palestine.[24] Richard Bauckham has drawn up charts of the relative frequency of different Jewish personal names in Palestine.[25] For this purpose he looks at sources including Josephus, the Dead Sea Scrolls, early rabbinic texts, and ossuaries (boxes of bones of the deceased). The chronological boundaries of his investigation are from 330 BC to AD 200, but in fact the vast bulk of the data comes from 50 BC to AD 135. Bauckham also excludes clearly fictional characters.[26]

For Jews in Palestine, Bauckham finds "2953 occurrences of 521 names, comprising 2625 occurrences of 447 male names and 328 occurrences of 74 female names."[27] He lists the six most popular Palestinian Jewish names as shown in table 3.6.[28]

---

24. Margaret H. Williams, "Palestinian Jewish Personal Names in Acts," in *The Book of Acts in Its First Century Setting*, vol. 4, *Palestinian Setting*, ed. Richard Bauckham (Grand Rapids, MI: Eerdmans, 1995), 79–113; Tal Ilan, *Lexicon of Jewish Names in Late Antiquity*, pt. 1, *Palestine 330 BCE–200 CE* (Tübingen: Mohr Siebeck, 2002).

25. Richard Bauckham, *Jesus and the Eyewitnesses: The Gospels as Eyewitness Testimony* (Grand Rapids, MI: Eerdmans, 2006), 67–92.

26. Bauckham, *Jesus and the Eyewitnesses*, 68–71.

27. Bauckham, *Jesus and the Eyewitnesses*, 71.

28. I am grateful to Professor Bauckham for sharing with me updated and more specific statistics on personal names, which he will soon publish. His new analysis focuses on names from 50 BC to AD 135 and finds that the relative order of the top eleven Palestinian Jewish male names is the same as in his *Jesus and the Eyewitnesses*, 85, with the following changes: Judah (Judas) and Eleazar swap positions to third and fourth places, respectively; Hananiah and Joshua swap to sixth and seventh places, respectively; Mattithiah and Jonathan are tied for eighth. Of course, we should expect that such statistics will change in small ways as new textual material comes to light. In the main text of this book, I follow Bauckham's published figures except where noted.

Table 3.6. Popular Jewish names in Palestine

Name	Occurrences in All Sources*	Number of NT Individuals
Simon	243	8
Joseph	218	6
Eleazar (Lazarus)	166	1
Judah	164	5
Yohanan	122	5
Joshua	99	2

* Bauckham, *Jesus and the Eyewitnesses*, 70. These numbers include the New Testament occurrences.

We can see that there is a fairly good correlation.[29] Bauckham also shows that, particularly among male names for which there are more data, the percentages of names in the Gospels and Acts are very similar to those across all the data sources for the period, approaching their closest when we look at the nine most popular male names, which is the largest data set in table 3.7.[30]

Table 3.7. Correlation of names by percentages per category

	Palestinian Jews	Gospels/Acts
Men with the two most popular names, Simon or Joseph	15.6%	18.2%
Men with one of the nine most popular names	41.5%	40.3%
Women with the two most popular names, Mary or Salome	28.6%	38.9%
Women with one of the nine most popular names	49.7%	61.1%

There were many Jews in Egypt at the time of the New Testament. For instance, in the great city of Alexandria two of the

---

29. I am not here claiming a formal statistical correlation.
30. Bauckham, *Jesus and the Eyewitnesses*, 71–72.

five quarters were called "Jewish" because of the considerable number of Jewish inhabitants.[31] However, in table 3.8, which follows Bauckham, Jews in Egypt had a very different set of names as found in Jewish inscriptions from there.[32]

Table 3.8. Frequency of particular Jewish names in Egypt versus Palestine*

Name	Rank in Egypt	Rank in Palestine
Eleazar	1	3
Sabbataius	2	68=
Joseph	3	2
Dositheus	4=	16
Pappus	4=	39=
Ptolemaius	6=	50=
Samuel	6=	23

* An equal sign indicates a tie in ranking.

Whether we look at Jews in Libya[33] or in western Turkey,[34] their patterns of names were quite different from those in Palestine. Rome had many Jews, but unlike those from Palestine, their names were mainly Greek or Latin, with only a tiny fraction being Hebrew or Aramaic.[35] The distinctions in names between locations are multifaceted, with different high- and low-frequency names for both males and

---

31. Philo, *In Flaccum* 55.

32. Data from Bauckham, *Jesus and the Eyewitnesses*, 73. We could similarly see contrasting names in Edfu in southern Egypt. See Margaret H. Williams, *The Jews among the Greeks and Romans: A Diasporan Sourcebook* (London: Duckworth, 1998), 101–3.

33. Williams, *Jews among the Greeks and Romans*, 29–30; Gert Lüderitz, *Corpus jüdischer Zeugnisse aus der Cyrenaika* (Wiesbaden: Reichert, 1983), esp. 147–59.

34. Williams, *Jews among the Greeks and Romans*, 166–67; J. Reynolds and R. Tannenbaum, *Jews and God-fearers at Aphrodisias* (Cambridge: Cambridge Philological Society, 1987), 97–105.

35. Harry Joshua Leon, "The Names of the Jews of Ancient Rome," *Transactions and Proceedings of the American Philological Association* 59 (1928): 205–24; and Joan Goodnick Westenholz, *The Jewish Presence in Ancient Rome* (Jerusalem: Bible Lands Museum, 1994), 101–17, 123–28.

females, for different languages, and for names unique to each location.

In other words, someone living in another part of the Roman Empire would not simply be able to think of Jewish names familiar to him and put them into a story, resulting in a plausible group of names for Palestinian Jews.

Disambiguation

Bauckham highlights a further feature, which is the ambiguity that arises when so many individuals share the same name, for example, Simon. He documents eleven different ways that ambiguity was avoided. Common ways of removing ambiguity included adding an element such as a father's name, a profession, or a place of origin.[36] This is what we find in the Gospels: disambiguators are used with the most common names and not with the less common ones.

The most common name for Palestinian Jewish males was Simon, so the Simons we have in the Gospels are often introduced with a disambiguator, such as Simon *Peter* (Mark 3:16), Simon *the Zealot* (Mark 3:18), Simon *the Leper* (Mark 14:3), and Simon *the Cyrenian* (Mark 15:21)—whose son's ossuary, incidentally, may well have been discovered.[37] Likewise Mary was the most common female name, and Marys are therefore disambiguated, as in "Mary *Magdalene* and Mary *the mother of James and Joseph*" (Matthew 27:56).

This level of knowledge of naming patterns has implications for the authorship of the Gospels. Someone living outside the land would not likely give people the right names. However, the Gospels have four different authors, each one of whom has managed to present us with a credible array of Palestinian

---

36. Bauckham, *Jesus and the Eyewitnesses*, 78–84.
37. Craig A. Evans, *Jesus and the Remains of His Day: Studies in Jesus and the Evidence of Material Culture* (Peabody, MA: Hendrickson, 2015), 31, 63–65.

Jewish names. What is more, they have disambiguated the most common names for that land even though in another land those same names were not so common as to require disambiguation.

The remarkable extent of this may be seen by considering the list of disciples as given in Matthew's Gospel. I have added in brackets the rank of these names for Palestinian Jewish men as given by Bauckham:[38]

> The names of the twelve apostles are these: first, Simon [1], who is called Peter, and Andrew [>99] his brother; James [11] the son of Zebedee, and John [5] his brother; Philip [61=] and Bartholomew [50=]; Thomas [>99] and Matthew [9] the tax collector; James [11] the son of Alphaeus, and Thaddaeus [39=]; Simon [1] the Zealot, and Judas [4] Iscariot, who betrayed him. (Matthew 10:2–4)

We see immediately that the more popular names, like Simon, Judas, Matthew, and James, have disambiguators, or, in the case of John, have clear contextual disambiguation (the name of his father). Disambiguators are used for the most popular eleven names. On the other hand, we have several names that, on Bauckham's rankings, are tied for thirty-ninth or lower in frequency: Thaddaeus, Bartholomew, Philip, and Thomas, which does not even make the top ninety-nine names. None of these have disambiguators.[39] So not only are the names authentically Palestinian, but the disambiguation patterns are such as would be necessary *in Palestine, but not elsewhere*. From this we may conclude that, wherever Matthew's Gospel was written, this list itself most likely took something close to its current form in Palestine.

---

38. Bauckham, *Jesus and the Eyewitnesses*, 85–88. The symbol > indicates a ranking beyond the number shown.

39. Of course, Andrew is a rare name and is contextually disambiguated, but this is only to explain his relationship with Simon Peter.

Contrast with Later Gospels—Names

The ability of the four Gospels to give plausible names for the people they mention can be contrasted with the poor job done within apocryphal Gospels. The second-century *Gospel of Thomas* is the most informed and mentions James the Just, Jesus, Mary, Matthew, Salome, Simon Peter, and, of course, Thomas.[40] However, the *Gospel of Mary*, also from the second century, has just five names: Andrew, Levi, Mary, Peter, and the Savior. Though Mary was the most common Palestinian Jewish female name, the *Gospel of Mary* does not even tell us which of the various Marys was supposed to be the author. Notice also that it is written at a stage sufficiently removed from Jesus that it no longer even called him *Jesus* by name. The term *the Savior* is obviously a later substitution.

From the same century we also have the *Gospel of Judas*. This has just two names suitable for Palestinian Jewish men: Judas and Jesus! However, it introduces a great many names, not at all Palestinian in nature, which seem to be a collection of sometimes garbled combinations of names from the Greek Bible and contemporary mysticism: Adam, Adamas, Adonaios, Barbelo, Eve = Zoe, Gabriel, Galila, Harmathoth, Michael, Nebro, Saklas, Seth, Sophia, Yaldabaoth, and Yobel.

Disambiguation in Speech

The disambiguation of names occurs not only in narrative but also in speech. Consider the references to John the Baptist in Matthew 14:1–11:

> At that time Herod the tetrarch heard about the fame of Jesus, and he said to his servants, "This is *John the Baptist*. He has been raised from the dead; that is why these miraculous

---

40. He is called the unlikely Didymos Judas Thomas "twin Judas twin" in the prologue of the Coptic version—the only complete version of the prologue or the whole.

powers are at work in him." For Herod had seized *John* and bound him and put him in prison for the sake of Herodias, his brother Philip's wife, because *John* had been saying to him, "It is not lawful for you to have her." And though he wanted to put him to death, he feared the people, because they held him to be a prophet. But when Herod's birthday came, the daughter of Herodias danced before the company and pleased Herod, so that he promised with an oath to give her whatever she might ask. Prompted by her mother, she said, "Give me the head of *John the Baptist* here on a platter." And the king was sorry, but because of his oaths and his guests he commanded it to be given. He sent and had *John* beheaded in the prison, and his head was brought on a platter and given to the girl, and she brought it to her mother.

In this passage John the Baptist is named five times. Twice he is called *John the Baptist* and thrice simply *John*. The three uses of *John* are by the narrator, and the two uses of *John the Baptist* are by a character in the narrative. There is a certain logic to this. If Herod had really heard about Jesus and said to his courtiers, "This is John," their reply would naturally have been "Which John?" It was the fifth most common name in Palestine, according to Bauckham's figures. Therefore, Herod would have needed to specify which John he meant. Matthew duly reports that this is what the tetrarch did (14:2). However, in verses 3 and 4 the identity of the person discussed is already clear. Therefore, it is sufficient for the narrator simply to speak of "John." Then, in verse 8, Herodias's daughter is reported to have asked for the head of John the Baptist in response to Herod's offer of a special favor. Here she names him in full: "John the Baptist." Imagine if she had not! How would anyone have known which John to behead? In verse 10 the narrator duly reports that Herod sent and beheaded "John."

Thus, we see that the narrator and the characters in the narrative are clearly distinguished. The characters speak exactly the way characters would have had to speak in that context in order to be clear. There are two simple explanations: the writer either reported just what people said or was so sophisticated as to be able to imitate the way people *would have spoken* in that historical context. Either way, the author must have had detailed cultural knowledge of the situation he was writing about.

The Name Jesus

A further illustration of the same feature involves the naming of Jesus. The name *Jesus* is an alternative form of the Old Testament name *Joshua* and was the sixth or seventh most common Palestinian Jewish male name, according to Bauckham.[41] As a popular name, if used without adequate contextual indications it would obviously have prompted the question "Which Jesus?" However, after Christianity had grown considerably, this would no longer have been the case. Jesus was famous. The name Jesus would have undergone a transformation rather like the very different and ill-fated name *Adolf*. A casual mention of that name in Germany in 1900 would have naturally elicited the question "Which Adolf?" There were many. But in 1945, Adolf Hitler would have been the one person immediately thought of.

Though the name *Jesus* was not so ill-fated, the analogy remains: in AD 30 that was a common and undistinctive name for a Jew in Palestine. But over time it became particularly associated with one individual, and its use for others declined.[42] We will see, however, that the Gospels all treat *Jesus* as a name sometimes needing an extra identifier.

---

41. Bauckham, *Jesus and the Eyewitnesses*, 70, gives this as sixth, but see note 28, above.
42. On its declining use, see Margaret Williams, "Palestinian Jewish Personal Names in Acts," 87.

In Matthew. We begin with the passage containing Matthew's first spoken use of the name *Jesus*, in a crowd setting:

> The disciples went and did as *Jesus* had directed them. They brought the donkey and the colt and put on them their cloaks, and he sat on them. Most of the crowd spread their cloaks on the road, and others cut branches from the trees and spread them on the road. And the crowds that went before him and that followed him were shouting, "Hosanna to the Son of David! Blessed is he who comes in the name of the Lord! Hosanna in the highest!" And when he entered Jerusalem, the whole city was stirred up, saying, "Who is this?" And the crowds said, "This is *the prophet Jesus, from Nazareth of Galilee*."
>
> And *Jesus* entered the temple and drove out all who sold and bought in the temple, and he overturned the tables of the money-changers and the seats of those who sold pigeons. (Matthew 21:6–12)

We see instantly that the narrator can call him just *Jesus*, which is entirely unambiguous in the context of the book. The crowds, however, cannot merely say, "This is Jesus." That would have been unclear. So they disambiguate by giving his place of origin. This is what would have had to happen if the event really took place.

Now consider the descriptions in Matthew 26:

> But *Jesus* remained silent. And the high priest said to him, "I adjure you by the living God, tell us if you are the Christ, the Son of God." *Jesus* said to him, "You have said so. But I tell you, from now on you will see the Son of Man seated at the right hand of Power and coming on the clouds of heaven." Then the high priest tore his robes and said, "He has uttered blasphemy. What further witnesses do we need? You have now heard his blasphemy. What is your

judgment?" They answered, "He deserves death." Then they spit in his face and struck him. And some slapped him, saying, "Prophesy to us, you Christ! Who is it that struck you?"

Now Peter was sitting outside in the courtyard. And a servant girl came up to him and said, "You also were with *Jesus the Galilean*." But he denied it before them all, saying, "I do not know what you mean." And when he went out to the entrance, another servant girl saw him, and she said to the bystanders, "This man was with *Jesus of Nazareth*." And again he denied it with an oath: "I do not know the man." After a little while the bystanders came up and said to Peter, "Certainly you too are one of them, for your accent betrays you." Then he began to invoke a curse on himself and to swear, "I do not know the man." And immediately the rooster crowed. And Peter remembered the saying of *Jesus*, "Before the rooster crows, you will deny me three times." And he went out and wept bitterly. (26:63–75)

The contrast here is between the simple naming of Jesus by the narrator in verses 63, 64, and 75, and the fuller naming of him by two different servant girls in the courtyard outside where Jesus is being interrogated by the high priest. The servant girls rightly accuse Peter of being one of Jesus's followers, but it would have been quite insufficient for them in a real setting to say, "You were with Jesus," since in all likelihood there would have been more than one Jesus at the high priest's residence that night.

Continuing in Matthew we find Pilate addressing the crowd and asking, "Whom do you want me to release for you: Barabbas or *Jesus who is called Christ*?" (27:17).[43] He

---

43. According to a less well attested manuscript reading, Pilate calls the criminal "Jesus Barabbas" rather than "Barabbas." Even if this is the correct reading, it only strengthens my argument that Jesus was a name in need of disambiguation.

asks again, "What shall I do with *Jesus who is called Christ*?" (27:22). The wording above Jesus's cross is said to have read, "This is *Jesus, the King of the Jews*" (27:37), and the angel who meets the women visiting Jesus's tomb says, "I know that you seek *Jesus who was crucified*" (28:5). In each case there is a disambiguator.

In Mark. The same occurs in Mark: there are disambiguators with the name *Jesus* in speech and not normally otherwise. Demons ask, "What have you to do with us, *Jesus of Nazareth*?" (1:24). The servant girl says to Peter, "You also were with *the Nazarene, Jesus*" (14:67), and the young man in a white robe (i.e., angel) says to the women at the tomb, "You seek *Jesus of Nazareth*" (16:6). A particularly interesting example has a disambiguator both outside and inside speech. Concerning the blind beggar Bartimaeus, Mark says that when he heard "that it was *Jesus of Nazareth*, he began to cry out and say, '*Jesus, Son of David*'" (10:47). The disambiguator is used outside speech because the narrative here is reporting what the blind man *heard*. Simply saying that someone with a common male name was passing by would not explain why the beggar began to call out.

In Luke. The same pattern of using disambiguators with the name *Jesus* occurs in speech in Luke:

- "Jesus of Nazareth" (4:34)
- "Jesus, Son of the Most High God" (8:28)
- "Jesus, Master" (17:13)
- "Jesus of Nazareth" (24:19)

We also have the same phenomenon as in the Mark 10:47 parallel when Luke reports about the blind beggar: "They told him, '*Jesus of Nazareth* is passing by.' And he cried out, '*Jesus,*

Son of David, have mercy on me'" (Luke 18:37–38). Again, if this event really took place, specifying *which* Jesus was meant would have been absolutely necessary.

In what might appear to be an exception in Luke, one instance of speech uses no disambiguator. The brigand on the cross next to Jesus turns to him and says, "*Jesus*, remember me" (Luke 23:42). However, the lack of disambiguator is not problematic, since these words come not in a typical crowd setting but in a personal address by someone on a cross, for whom every word must require considerable effort.

In John. Finally, we find the same pattern in John's Gospel. When speech is reported, we get disambiguation:

- "Jesus of Nazareth, the son of Joseph" (1:45)
- "Jesus, the son of Joseph" (6:42)
- "Jesus of Nazareth" (18:5)
- "Jesus of Nazareth" (18:7)

We find it also in the writing above the cross: "Jesus of Nazareth, the King of the Jews" (19:19). There is, however, an exception in John's Gospel. In 9:11 the man born blind, who has been given his sight by Jesus, is asked who healed him. He replies simply, "The man called *Jesus.*" However, even this bare description actually reinforces the pattern. Those most familiar with the writing style of this Gospel in fact believe that the man's ignorance is being portrayed. The fact that he is only able to identify Jesus as a man possessing a high-frequency name and does not know more about him fits exactly with the narrative's portrayal of him as knowing little at this stage, though he soon comes to know much more.[44]

---

44. See, for instance, Barnabas Lindars, *The Gospel of John* (London: Marshall, Morgan & Scott, 1972), 345.

What Names Tell Us

One notable feature about names is that they are often difficult
to remember. This is hardly surprising since most human names
are assigned rather arbitrarily. There is usually no memorable
reason why an individual should be called one of the many
names that are conventional within a given culture. So we regularly forget names even as we remember many other things
about people. In social settings we can often recall details of
the last conversation we had with someone even as we struggle
to remember his or her name. We watch a film and remember
its characters and what they did, but often forget the names
of those characters. Stories, as coherent threads, are easier to
remember than names as arbitrary labels.

This has implications for the *quality* of information we have
within the Gospels. We have already seen converging lines of
evidence suggesting that the Gospel writers were highly familiar with the places they wrote about. Their knowledge of local
names reinforces this pattern of local familiarity. It is quite unlikely that any of the writers, if living outside the land, would
have been able simply to research local naming patterns and
thereby write a plausible narrative. It is beyond improbable to
think that *four* authors might have been able to do this, as each
contains names not in the other three.

But let us suppose the Gospel writers *were* natives of the
land and, knowing what people were generally called, made up
names for their stories accordingly. Even in this situation we
would hardly expect that when we combine the work of the
four individual authors, we would find the frequencies of the
names in correct proportions to those used locally.

Time and again we are surprised when we read surveys of
the most common names today. This is because our intuitions
of what names are most common are built upon the relatively

small sample of people we meet. The intuition of a single locally informed writer would be unlikely to enable him or her to produce names for fictional characters that would ring true. It is even less likely that four such writers could.

By far the simplest explanation is that the Gospel authors were able to give an authentic pattern of names in their narrative because they were reliably reporting what people were actually called. Given that names are also hard to remember, the authentic pattern of names in the Gospels suggests that their testimony is of *high quality*. After all, if they have correctly remembered the *less* memorable details—the names of individuals—then they should have had no difficulty in remembering the *more* memorable outline of events.

I have often heard the transmission of stories about Jesus likened to what Americans call the telephone game and elsewhere in the English-speaking world is known, unfortunately, as Chinese whispers. The game offers enjoyment in how much a message is corrupted when whispered successively round a group of people. It is just this ease of message corruption that Bart Ehrman appeals to when he asks:

> What do you suppose happened to the stories [about Jesus] over the years, as they were told and retold, not as disinterested news stories reported by eyewitnesses but as propaganda meant to convert people to faith, told by people who had themselves heard them fifth- or sixth- or nineteenth-hand? Did you or your kids ever play the telephone game at a birthday party?[45]

The analogy is, however, ill-chosen. After all, this game is specifically *optimized to produce corruption*. Hence come the rules

---

45. Bart D. Ehrman, *Jesus, Interrupted: Revealing the Hidden Contradictions in the Bible (and Why We Don't Know about Them)* (New York: HarperOne, 2009), 146–47.

that one must whisper, passing on the message only once and only to a single person, and there must be sufficient people playing to ensure that the message is corrupted.

The circumstances surrounding the passing on of reliable information in the Gospels could not be more different. Not only are the names of people and places authentic, showing that they could not have been passed through multiple unreliable steps in transmission, but the very conditions in early Christianity were unsuitable for producing corruption: they were marked by a high emphasis on truth, a sense of authoritative teaching, a wide geographical spread among followers of Jesus, and a high personal cost to following him. A plausible scenario for accidental corruption simply was not there. By contrast, the view that people passed on reliable information explains the data more simply.

Other Signs of Knowledge

In addition to broad knowledge of geography and personal names, many other features reveal the knowledge of the Gospel authors and therefore give us clues to their identities. Here are a few examples.

Jewishness

Scholars disagree on many matters concerning the Gospels, but on one thing they seem almost universally agreed—the Gospels are Jewish.

Matthew, after beginning with a sixteen-verse genealogy in a style characteristic of the Old Testament, contains about fifty-five quotations from the Jewish Scriptures,[46] and through-

---

46. Craig L. Blomberg, "Matthew," in *Commentary on the New Testament Use of the Old Testament*, ed. G. K. Beale and D. A. Carson (Grand Rapids, MI: Baker Academic, 2007), 1.

out is dealing with Jewish customs, debates, language, and politics.

Mark begins with a quotation from the Old Testament (1:2–3) and contains a series of five controversy stories essentially about Jewish debates over who can forgive sins, with whom one can eat, fasting, and (two narratives) the Sabbath (2:1–3:6). Jesus's main speeches involve parables (chap. 4), what makes one unclean (chap. 7), and the end of the age (chap. 13)—in other words, a Jewish genre, a Jewish interest, and a text full of Jewish apocalyptic language.[47]

John begins with the same two words as the earliest Greek translation of the Old Testament and with an opening highly reflective of the beginning of the Bible. John knows about the stone vessels for purification, which are characteristically Jewish (John 2:6).[48]

Arguably the *least* Jewish Gospel is Luke, but in it we find a strikingly detailed knowledge of Jewish thought. For instance, when Jesus is having his dispute with the Devil (Luke 4:9–12; also reported in Matthew 4:5–7) the matter under discussion is the correct interpretation of Psalm 91. The discovery of one of the Dead Sea Scrolls (called 11Q11), which shows that this psalm was particularly used to exorcise demons, gives a new depth to our understanding of this interaction. Luke's Gospel has recorded something that exactly fits with the Judaism of the time.[49] Similarly, knowledge of Jewish thought is shown when Luke alone reports that Jesus died saying, "Father, into your hands I commit my spirit!" (Luke 23:46)—a direct quotation

---

47. Daniel Boyarin, *The Jewish Gospels: The Story of the Jewish Christ* (New York: New Press, 2012), 68–69, comments on the debates in Mark 2 and 7: "Jesus, or Mark, certainly knew his way around a halakhic argument."

48. Stuart S. Miller, *At the Intersection of Texts and Material Finds: Stepped Pools, Stone Vessels, and Ritual Purity among the Jews of Roman Galilee* (Göttingen: Vandenhoeck & Ruprecht, 2015), 155.

49. Evans, *Jesus and the Remains of His Day*, 92, 106–8.

from Psalm 31:5, which R. Steven Notley calls "the traditional deathbed prayer of an observant Jew."[50]

Implications of the Gospels' Jewishness for Their Dates

Christianity began as a subdivision of Judaism—all the first Christians were Jews. However, within a few decades large numbers of Gentiles were becoming Christians. One thing on which Christian and non-Christian sources agree is the rapid growth of Christianity.

It was only natural that gradually the original Jewishness of Christianity was largely forgotten. Scholars debate the timing of the process, but there is no doubt that Christianity and Judaism parted ways. In general, the later the Christian text, the less it resembles other forms of Judaism. If we start with texts we know can be dated to the second century or later, they look decidedly less Jewish than the four Gospels. For example, we can compare the four Gospels with the *Gospel of Thomas*, which is from the mid-second century. As is typical for something written in that period, the *Gospel of Thomas* reflects little Jewish background.[51]

The Jewishness of the four Gospels is most easily explained if they are early and reflect early ideas. Early is a relative term, but a momentous change must have taken place in Judaism after the Jewish war with the Romans (AD 66–73) devastated the Jewish populations of Judaea and Galilee and led to the destruction of the Jerusalem temple and the end of Jerusalem as the Jewish capital. Scholars divide over whether they should date the Gospels before or after the destruction of Jerusalem in AD 70, but we have seen already that many scholars hold Matthew and Luke to have been written after the destruction

---

50. Notley, *In the Master's Steps*, 77.
51. S. J. Gathercole, *The Gospel of Thomas: Introduction and Commentary* (Leiden: Brill, 2014), 163–64.

of Jerusalem, while some place Mark in the period leading up to that event, and some after.

One reason scholars are inclined to date Matthew, Mark, or Luke after AD 70 is that these Gospels have Jesus speaking of the destruction of the Jerusalem temple and related events (Matthew 24:2; Mark 13:2; Luke 21:6, 20, 24). Obviously if one does not believe in supernatural prediction, one has to date these references no earlier than when the destruction of the temple could either be naturally predicted or have already occurred. But if we allow the possibility of miraculous prediction, we are not so limited.

We might put it like this: the four Gospels are so influenced by Judaism in their outlook, subject matter, and detail that it would be reasonable to date them considerably before the Jewish War.

Now, I am not saying that all of the Gospels were written before this date, or even that any was. My argument is that their reliability is compelling, given a variety of possible dates and a range of possible interrelationships between them. The Jewishness of the material favors earlier dates at least for their content, so that even if we say that the Gospels are late first century, the material in them is not.

Botanical Terms

The Gospels also mention an array of botanical terms, many of which could fit with anywhere round the Mediterranean. Figs, vines, and wheat grew in every country and do not help us pin down the context of the narratives. However, Jesus's saying about how the Pharisees were careful to tithe their mint, dill, and cumin (Matthew 23:23) shows specific knowledge of the rabbinic debates about tithing of dill and cumin.[52]

---

52. Mishnah *Maaseroth* 4.5 and *Eduyoth* 5.3. See Herbert Danby, *The Mishnah, Translated from the Hebrew with Introduction and Brief Explanatory Notes* (Oxford: Oxford University Press, 1933), 72, 431. On the identity of the plants, see my comments

Another striking piece of knowledge appears where Luke records that the tax collector Zacchaeus climbed up a sycamore tree in Jericho (Luke 19:4). The relevant species, *Ficus sycomorus*, did not grow in northern Mediterranean countries (Italy, Greece, Turkey), and in fact lacks natural pollinators in those countries.[53] But this tree was characteristic of Jericho, according to the second-century rabbi Abba Shaul.[54] How did the author know there were sycamores in Jericho? The simple explanation is that he had either been there or spoken to someone who had.

Finance

Matthew and Mark place a whole group of tax collectors in Capernaum (Matthew 9:9–10; Mark 2:14–15). What is not mentioned in any Gospel is that Capernaum was at a strategic point at the northern end of the Sea of Galilee, and a key location for collecting customs on what crossed the border of the territory of Herod Antipas. Likewise, Luke mentions Zacchaeus as being a *chief* tax collector in Jericho (Luke 19:2). It is not only the sycamore tree that fits the location. Jericho was also the major town on Pontius Pilate's side of the border of Judaea with Peraea, the territory of Herod Antipas. So Matthew and Mark, on the one hand, and Luke, on the other, have independently recorded *different* events with tax collectors in *different* border towns. The Gospels show knowledge of the local tax systems.

Matthew himself was traditionally identified as a tax collector, and Matthew's Gospel shows the greatest level of financial interest, including numerous references to money and treasure that Matthew alone records:

---

in Peter M. Head and P. J. Williams, "Q Review," *Tyndale Bulletin* 54, no. 1 (2003): 136–38.

53. J. Galil and D. Eisikowitch, "On the Pollination Ecology of Ficus Sycomorus in East Africa," *Ecology* 49, no. 2 (1968): 260.

54. Babylonian Talmud *Pesachim* 57a.

- The magi, with their rich gifts (2:11)
- The parable about hidden treasure (13:44)
- The parable about the discovered pearl (13:45–46)
- The scribe compared to someone bringing out old and new treasures (13:52)
- The account of Peter and the temple tax collectors (17:24–27)
- The parable of the servant who was forgiven a huge debt of ten thousand talents and who refused to forgive a fellow servant a debt of a hundred denarii (18:23–35)
- The parable of the workers in the vineyard, discontented with their pay of one denarius for a day because the same was given to late arrivals who had worked less time (20:1–16)
- The parable about talents (25:14–30)[55]
- Judas's betrayal money (27:3) and what was purchased with it (27:7)
- The bribe given by the chief priests to the guards at Jesus's tomb (28:12)

Both Matthew and Mark mention *corban* (Matthew 27:6; Mark 7:11), the dedication of money to the temple. But they record different incidents: one a speech by the chief priests and another an occasion of Jesus quoting others. And the two Gospels even spell the word differently, showing their independence in knowing the term.[56]

Local Languages

There is evidence for the use of Greek, Hebrew, and Aramaic in Palestine at the time of Jesus. The exact ratio of speakers of each language and the extent of multilingualism are debated.

---

55. Luke has a similar story about a smaller currency, the mina (Luke 19:12–27).
56. See also Josephus, *Jewish War* 2.175; Mishnah *Nedarim* 2.2.

However, we see clear indications that Matthew, Mark, and John had some familiarity with the local languages.

Matthew 21:9, Mark 11:9–10, and John 12:13 record the crowd near Passover time calling out "hosanna" to Jesus, and Matthew 21:15 even states that this cry was later taken up by children. The word originally meant "save" and came from Psalm 118:25. The Gospels' use of this word is highly appropriate since it came from near the climax of six psalms sung during Passover. However, two further points deserve note.

1. In the Gospels *hosanna* is not used in a sense of "save." The expressions "Hosanna in the highest!" (Matthew 21:9; Mark 11:10) and "Hosanna to the Son of David!" (Matthew 21:9, 15) do not make much sense if the word still means "save." It is clearly a word the crowd likes, but it has shifted to express celebration. This shift of the meaning of *hosanna* shows up in later Jewish sources. Thus, the writers show knowledge not only of this word's use by Jews at a particular time but also of its development over time.

2. In the Gospels *hosanna* has a different form from that in the original Hebrew, which was *hoshianna*. The *s* is used for *sh* simply because Greek cannot express the Hebrew *sh* sound. But the omission of the *i* sound represents a linguistic change over time, reflecting the Hebrew at the time of the New Testament, not when the psalm was written. The Gospel writers have the word exactly as it was pronounced in the first century even though this is not the sort of knowledge any author could obtain simply by consulting books.[57]

---

57. A fuller explanation is this: Earlier Hebrew had a longer and shorter form of the imperative of some verbs in the masculine singular. *Hoshia* is the longer form, and *hosha* the shorter form. The final *nna* is made up of a separate particle *na* preceded by a reinforcing *n*. Over time, the longer form of the imperative was entirely dropped. See also the short form *hoshana*, used in a sense quite different from the original in a fourth-century quotation in the Babylonian Talmud *Sukkah* 37b.

Unusual Customs

The Gospels bear witness to a variety of unusual or local customs. While any one of these might have become known more widely, their combination suggests deep local awareness. I will merely provide a few examples from the days leading up to Jesus's crucifixion.

Matthew and Mark present Jesus as lodging in the village of Bethany, less than two miles from Jerusalem, in the days preceding the Passover (Matthew 26:6; Mark 11:11, 19), but making arrangements to celebrate the Passover in Jerusalem itself (Matthew 26:17–18; Mark 14:12–14) and then going out to the Mount of Olives (Matthew 26:30; Mark 14:26). Luke has him lodging overnight on the Mount of Olives (Bethany was on its eastern slope), but coming into Jerusalem on the day of the Passover meal and then going out to the Mount of Olives, though seemingly not to the usual place of his overnight lodging (Luke 21:37; 22:7–8, 39). John mentions his arrival at Bethany six days before the Passover but does not record that he came into Jerusalem for his final evening meal. However, this is implied by the fact that he and his disciples afterward crossed the Kidron valley toward a garden, which fits with the depiction in the other Gospels of Jesus leaving Jerusalem for the Mount of Olives (John 12:1; 18:1).

The Gospels thus present a common picture, though in different ways, presupposing the custom that it was necessary for the Passover to be celebrated within the walls of Jerusalem.[58] Then Matthew 26:30 and Mark 14:26 make particular mention that Jesus and the disciples sang a hymn before going to the Mount of Olives. According to rabbinic tradition, the Hallel (Psalms 113–118) had to be sung at the Passover feast.[59]

---

58. Mishnah *Pesachim* 7.9, 12 and discussion in Notley, *In the Master's Steps*, 65.
59. Mishnah *Pesachim* 9.3 and discussion in Notley, *In the Master's Steps*, 69.

Interestingly, neither Matthew nor Mark points out any connection between the disciples' hymn and the crowd's cry of "hosanna," from Psalm 118:25, which both had mentioned a few verses earlier. It is only our knowledge of Jewish traditions outside the Gospels that allows us to see the link.

While in the garden of Gethsemane, Jesus is approached by a band of people from the chief priests coming to arrest him. They are described in the Synoptic Gospels as carrying clubs (Matthew 26:47, 55; Mark 14:43, 48; Luke 22:52). A rabbinic source likewise describes the priests' servants as carrying clubs.[60]

Once arrested, Jesus appears before the high priest, who judges him to have blasphemed, and who therefore tears his clothes (Matthew 26:65; Mark 14:63–64), which is, again, something associated in rabbinic writing with a response to blasphemy.[61]

---

60. Babylonian Talmud *Pesachim* 57a. See also Evans, *Jesus and the Remains of His Day*, 157.

61. Babylonian Talmud *Moed Qatan* 26a.

4

Undesigned Coincidences

The Gospels show particular signs of authenticity that have been labeled *undesigned coincidences*. The Cambridge theology professor John James Blunt (1794–1855) crystallized a form of this argument,[1] and the same argument has been developed more recently by Lydia McGrew.[2] There is not space here to repeat these arguments, which can be read elsewhere, so I will content myself with just a few examples.

In an undesigned coincidence, writers show agreement of a kind that it is hard to imagine as deliberately contrived by either author to make the story look authentic. Often the agreement is so subtle and indirect that all but the most careful reader are likely to miss it. If you suppose that Gospel writers put in such agreements to make their narratives appear authentic, then you imagine that they are among the most brilliant of all ancient authors. The idea that several of the

---

1. J. J. Blunt, *Undesigned Coincidences in the Writings both of the Old and New Testament, An Argument of Their Veracity* (New York: Robert Carter, 1847).
2. Lydia McGrew, *Hidden in Plain View: Undesigned Coincidences in the Gospels and Acts* (Chillicothe, OH: DeWard, 2017).

Gospel writers might have done this independently is even less plausible.

Two Sisters

Let us consider two stories about the sisters Mary and Martha, recorded in Luke and John.[3] The two narratives are quite different. In John, most of a chapter is taken up with the account of Jesus raising Lazarus, brother of Mary and Martha, from the dead. In Luke we have the following narrative, with no obvious link to John:

> Now as they went on their way, Jesus entered a village. And a woman named Martha welcomed him into her house. And she had a sister called Mary, who sat at the Lord's feet and listened to his teaching. But Martha was distracted with much serving. And she went up to him and said, "Lord, do you not care that my sister has left me to serve alone? Tell her then to help me." But the Lord answered her, "Martha, Martha, you are anxious and troubled about many things, but one thing is necessary. Mary has chosen the good portion, which will not be taken away from her." (Luke 10:38–42)

Obviously, if John and Luke knew of each other's book, then they could have copied the names, but they certainly did not copy their completely different narratives.

Luke gives us a cameo of two contrasting characters: Martha, stressed about practicalities, and Mary, sitting, listening to Jesus's teaching and ignoring any of the concerns of her hardworking sister. It is easy to imagine these sisters as contrasting personality types: one an activist and the other more contemplative.

---

3. Luke 10:38–42; John 11:1–46.

In John we see the same two women after their brother has died. Jesus approaches their village. As soon as Martha hears, she goes to Jesus, while Mary "remained seated" at home (John 11:20). Immediately we see a coincidence in the Gospel descriptions, not of the event but of the types of responses. In both Luke and John, Mary sits while Martha acts. In both, Martha does the welcoming. After meeting Jesus, the ever-active Martha secretly sends a message to her sister that Jesus is calling her. Mary then gets up quickly, and those with her think she is going to weep at the tomb (John 11:31). Coming to Jesus, unlike her sister, "she fell at his feet" (John 11:32—recall that she was at Jesus's feet in Luke too). Jesus sees her weeping (John 11:33), though there is no similar record that Martha weeps. After arriving at the tomb and himself weeping, Jesus commands for the stone to be moved. At this point Martha says, "Lord, by this time there will be an odor, for he has been dead four days" (John 11:39). This extremely practical concern misses the point that Jesus is about to raise Lazarus from the dead.

What we see is this: there is no obvious reason to conclude that one author has copied the other, but the two narratives present the two characters in ways that accord with each other. This is so in the physical matters of Mary's "sitting" and positioning herself physically at Jesus's feet, but also in the practical concerns of Martha in both accounts. In both stories, she is also the more active. The easiest interpretation of this is that both Luke and John are describing true characters. This model accounts for a lot in a simple way. Other scenarios are possible, but they do not explain things so straightforwardly.

Two Brothers

Next we consider a brief coincidence about two brothers, recorded in Mark and Luke. Mark names Jesus's twelve disciples and says that Jesus nicknamed the brothers James and John "Sons of Thunder" (Mark 3:17). Nothing more is said in Mark as to what might have been Jesus's reason for this. Likewise, Matthew and John say nothing relevant. However, Luke records this incident:

> When the days drew near for him [Jesus] to be taken up, he set his face to go to Jerusalem. And he sent messengers ahead of him, who went and entered a village of the Samaritans, to make preparations for him. But the people did not receive him, because his face was set toward Jerusalem. And when his disciples James and John saw it, they said, *"Lord, do you want us to tell fire to come down from heaven and consume them?"* But he turned and rebuked them. (Luke 9:51–55)

Thus, the brothers called "Sons of Thunder" in Mark are recorded in Luke as wanting to call down lightning. The two reports fit well together, as one appears to record a name based on character, and the other appears to report a character fitting well with the name.

As we have seen, the passage about the two brothers is in Luke 9, and the one about the two sisters is in Luke 10. Luke 9 connects with Mark and Luke 10 with John. Both accounts in Luke pertain to character and present characters in ways that appear corroborated by other texts.

Of course, one could explain this away. One could imagine that Luke read the notice about "Sons of Thunder" in Mark and then built a story out of it. That would not explain Luke's knowledge of traveling routes in the surrounding passages or his awareness of tensions of Jews traveling through Samaritan areas. But even if Luke made up his narrative in Luke 9 based on Mark, that would not explain the relationship of Luke 10 to John's Gospel.

In McGrew's listing of undesigned coincidences, on nine occasions the Synoptic Gospels explain John, on six occasions

John explains the Synoptics, and on four occasions the Synoptics explain each other.[4] There are also other undesigned coincidences besides.[5] It is possible to explain away each one, but each new explanation adds complexity. The simple assumption that we are dealing with truthful records explains the textual phenomena with one stroke.

I find that the argument from undesigned coincidences seems to impress people less if they do not know the text well or if they consider only a few examples. It is a cumulative argument from simplicity. The complexity of alternative explanations therefore becomes apparent as more examples are considered.

Two Fish

We come now to consider the miraculous account in which Jesus fed five thousand men and also the women and children with them from just five loaves and two fish. It is in fact the only miracle, other than Jesus's resurrection, to be included in all four Gospels.

Both Mark and John comment on the grass in the setting of the miracle. Mark says that there was "green grass" (Mark 6:39), and John says that there was "much grass" (John 6:10). Neither makes anything more of this point, and one might wonder whether it is a detail put in to make the story look authentic. Mark explains that Jesus went to the remote location in order to get out of the way of the crowds. "And he said to them, 'Come away by yourselves to a desolate place and rest a while.' For many were coming and going, and they had no leisure even to eat" (Mark 6:31). This involves Jesus getting into a boat and going to a more desolate place. Mark does nothing more with the idea that many people were moving about.

---

4. McGrew, *Hidden in Plain View*, 62, 82, 97.
5. McGrew, *Hidden in Plain View*, 130.

However, John, and John alone, records that at the time of the miracle the Passover was approaching (John 6:4). This was the biggest Jewish festival of the year, when the largest number of pilgrims would travel to Jerusalem to attend. John records nothing about crowds traveling, and yet it is precisely the festival in John that would explain the detail in Mark about people traveling in such numbers. In Mark, the fact that Jesus moved locations indicates that it was not a mere increase in traffic for a few hours, but a more prolonged increase in movement of people such as normally occurred only at the time of festivals. This therefore is an undesigned coincidence between Mark and John. John explains a puzzle in Mark, and yet, according to almost all scholarly opinion, Mark came first.

Immediately after mentioning Passover, John records this:

> Lifting up his eyes, then, and seeing that a large crowd was coming toward him, Jesus said to Philip, "Where are we to buy bread, so that these people may eat?" He said this to test him, for he himself knew what he would do. Philip answered him, "Two hundred denarii worth of bread would not be enough for each of them to get a little." One of his disciples, Andrew, Simon Peter's brother, said to him, "There is a boy here who has five barley loaves and two fish, but what are they for so many?" (John 6:5–9)

John gives no explanation of why Jesus should single out Philip for this question, nor why Andrew should join in the reply. However, earlier John says, "Now Philip was from *Bethsaida*, the city of Andrew and Peter" (John 1:44; see also 12:21). John does nothing with this information, but it makes sense in the light of Luke 9:10, which locates the miracle near *Bethsaida*. This information impacts how we read John. If we read John on its own, we see no particular reason why Jesus should ask

Philip rather than any other of his disciples, nor why Philip and Andrew should be involved in responding to the problem Jesus has posed. However, once we plug in the information from Luke, the whole scene is explained: Jesus turns to a man with local knowledge, and he and another man with local knowledge are involved in replying.

So in this narrative, John explains the many people traveling in Mark, and Luke explains the dialogue in John. Even the little detail in John that the boy has barley loaves (John 6:9) fits nicely with the nearness of Passover, which immediately follows the barley harvest.

But we need to return to the initial detail in Mark and John about the grass. Would there really have been much of it, and would it really have been green? Figure 4.1 shows a rainfall chart for the nearby town of Tiberias.[6]

Figure 4.1. Tiberias precipitation

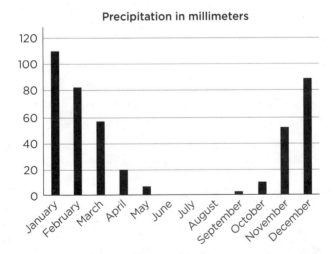

Precipitation in millimeters

---

6. Data from https://en.climate-data.org/location/28706/, accessed March 14, 2018.

Between the years AD 26 and 36, all possible dates for Passover ranged between the last days of March and the end of April. So if this event really took place at the time recorded, we should indeed expect that after the five most significant months of precipitation, grass would have been green.

Note, however, that none of our undesigned coincidences touches directly on the miracle. One might therefore be inclined to claim that the setting was realistic, but not the miracle. The miracle, someone might argue, arose as the story was told from one person to another and was exaggerated. But the problem with treating the central part of the story—the miracle—as careless exaggeration is that the undesigned coincidences suggest careful transmission of peripheral details. If transmission of the major elements of a story has been careless, we should not expect the minor elements to be well transmitted. Therefore, the idea that the miracle account arose through careless exaggeration involves an unrealistic process of *selective corruption of information* in the story. It lacks explanatory power for the current shape of the text.

Two Wives

The final undesigned coincidence I will mention is of a different sort: a coincidence between the Jewish historian Josephus and the Synoptic Gospels. We begin with Josephus, who explains how Jews widely viewed the defeat of Herod Antipas's army by his neighbor King Aretas IV of Nabatea in around AD 36.

> But to some of the Jews the destruction of Herod's army seemed to be divine vengeance, and certainly a just vengeance, for his treatment of John, surnamed the Baptist. For Herod had put him to death, though he was a good man and had exhorted the Jews to lead righteous lives, to practise justice towards their fellows and piety towards God, and

so doing to join in baptism. In his view this was a necessary preliminary if baptism was to be acceptable to God. They must not employ it to gain pardon for whatever sins they committed, but as a consecration of the body implying that the soul was already thoroughly cleansed by right behaviour. When others too joined the crowds about him, because they were aroused to the highest degree by his sermons, Herod became alarmed. Eloquence that had so great an effect on mankind might lead to some form of sedition, for it looked as if they would be guided by John in everything that they did. Herod decided therefore that it would be much better to strike first and be rid of him before his work led to an uprising, than to wait for an upheaval, get involved in a difficult situation and see his mistake. Though John, because of Herod's suspicions, was brought in chains to Machaerus, the stronghold that we have previously mentioned, and there put to death, yet the verdict of the Jews was that the destruction visited upon Herod's army was a vindication of John, since God saw fit to inflict such a blow on Herod.[7]

The account of John the Baptist contains many elements common to the Gospels, including his preaching to large crowds,[8] his emphasis on interpersonal justice,[9] his stress on the need for behavioral change prior to baptism,[10] and then his imprisonment and execution by Herod. There is, however, something odd about Josephus's account, namely, the lack of explanation for why people would specifically link John the Baptist's death with the defeat of Herod's army. This connection can be supplied only if we combine information from the Gospels and Josephus.

7. Josephus, *Antiquities* 18.116–19, Loeb Classical Library 433 (Cambridge, MA: Harvard University Press, 1965), 81–85.
8. Matthew 3:5; Mark 1:5; Luke 3:7.
9. Luke 3:10–14.
10. Matthew 3:2; Mark 1:15.

Josephus tells us that the cause of contention between Herod Antipas and Aretas was that Antipas had married Aretas's daughter Phasaelis and, after a long marriage, had divorced her in favor of Herodias, wife of Antipas's half-brother.[11]

The Gospels tell us that John the Baptist had publicly opposed Herod's new marriage (Matthew 14:4; Mark 6:18; Luke 3:19) and that this was the cause for his arrest. When we presuppose the information from the Gospels, Josephus's account makes more sense: the Jews connected the destruction of Herod's army with his execution of John the Baptist precisely because John's execution had been for publicly opposing the new marriage that was the root cause of the conflict. The simplest explanation is that we have basically true complementary accounts, each recording part of a larger body of events.

---

11. Josephus, *Antiquities* 18.110–15.

5

Do We Have Jesus's Actual Words?

Arguably, we have greater knowledge of what Jesus said than of sayings from any other ancient person who did not write a book. Often ancient writers present us with a single source for an ancient speech—Pericles's "Funeral Oration," in Thucydides; or Eleazar's pre-suicide speeches, in Josephus.[1] Occasionally we are fortunate to have more than one source of what someone said. For instance, with Socrates (d. 399 BC) we have two main sources, Plato and Xenophon, and scholars debate how much of what is attributed to Socrates actually goes back to him. But for Jesus, the Gospels give us an unusual combination of speeches and sayings of varying lengths, as well as numerous interactive scenes. Since all four Gospels record speech extensively and in a variety of complex inter-relationships, reports of Jesus's speech can be examined for signs of authenticity.

---

1. Thucydides, *Peloponnesian War* 2.35–46; Josephus, *Jewish War* 7.323–36, 341–88.

In the Gospels the bulk of Jesus's activity is set in Galilee or Jerusalem, with stays recorded in Judaea and some events whose locations are not entirely clear. Jesus is also reported to have visited Samaria (John 4:4), Peraea (Matthew 19:1), and the region near Tyre and Sidon (Mark 7:24). This chapter will argue that we have multiple reasons to trust the reports of what Jesus said in the Gospels, but before we consider those, we must first define what trustworthy reporting is.

Quotation and Memorization

Nowadays we use quotation marks to distinguish quoted words from their surroundings. Though having special signs to indicate speech is at least as old as the Hittites of the second millennium BC, our modern quotation marks are quite recent, originating only in the sixteenth century.[2] However, they change the way we think about quotation. They mark the beginning and the end of speech and, by doing so, introduce two rules into truthful reporting that simply did not exist before quotation marks were invented: they demand (1) that no words be omitted without indication (such as by ellipsis points) and (2) that no words can be added, modified, or substituted without indication (such as by square brackets). We must remember that when the Gospels were written, these two rules just did not exist. That means that we need to think ourselves back into a time when these two rules were not even considerations.

I regard this as the problem of *bounded quotations*. It is not that people in the ancient world did not have an idea of accurate quotation and were unable to quote verbatim. There is plenty of evidence of exact quotation, no different from our quotations today. But we do not have to think about it for long to recog-

---

2. Keith Houston, *Shady Characters: The Secret Life of Punctuation, Symbols and Other Typographical Marks* (London: Norton, 2013), 197–200.

nize that our modern conventions are rather constricting on truthful reporting, because in our culture we feel the need either to quote a whole sequence verbatim (in which case it must be within quotation marks) or else to paraphrase it, often trying *not* to use the exact words in order to avoid a charge of plagiarism. In practical terms, this also means that we have a rigid distinction between reporting direct speech ("she said, 'X'") and indirect speech ("she said that X"). Our weddedness to marking bounded quotations is mainly a product of our inability to think outside our writing conventions and must be set aside when we want to evaluate the truthfulness of an ancient report of speech.

Ancient truthful and responsible quotation did not need to observe our modern rule of marked boundaries. It was typically announced with a verb or particle introducing the speech and, unless explicitly claiming to be complete and verbatim, should be read in the knowledge that, in an ancient culture, truthful quotation granted certain freedoms in quotation not available to us.

This does not mean that truthful quotation could include just anything. Within Judaism we see plenty of interest in the memorization of what rabbis said. In fact, the period of approximately the first two centuries AD is commonly known within Judaism as the tannaitic period, named after the *tannaim*, plural of *tanna*, meaning one who memorized and taught the tradition of the oral law. Rabbinic confidence in memorization was so high that some rabbis even banned the writing of oral traditions.[3] Though we cannot be sure that all Jewish traditions which were later written down preserve information from before AD 70, scholars agree that the Mishnah (early third century), Jerusalem Talmud (early fifth century), Babylonian Talmud (early sixth century), and Masoretic vocalization

---

3. Babylonian Talmud *Temurah* 14b.

tradition (sixth to tenth centuries) preserve information from the first century.

The likelihood that Jesus's teaching was preserved is highlighted when we consider that all four Gospels present him as a formal teacher, with students (disciples). By my count there are 195 references in the Gospels to individuals or groups as his disciple(s). Forty-five times he is said to teach, forty times to be a teacher, and twelve times he is called rabbi. Luke alone, who more commonly avoids exclusively Jewish vocabulary, does not use the term *rabbi*. If Jesus really was a teacher or rabbi and had twelve special disciples, and if these terms are to have their normal meanings, then we would expect that a significant task of the disciples would have been to memorize specific sayings of their teacher.

The content of many of the sayings seems more likely to have been passed down rather than invented. Jesus often made statements that would have been tough for early Christians to stomach. In Matthew's Gospel he calls his followers "evil" (7:11), refers to Gentiles as "dogs" (15:26), tells his followers to do everything their frequent opponents the Pharisees say (23:3), and dies asking why God has forsaken him (27:46). Other Gospels are similarly embarrassing. Moreover, he does not say precisely what people might want him to say by giving guidance to those who will come later. He leaves no explicit instructions concerning what to do about non-Jews in the church, what to do about circumcision, or how to run a church meeting. These omissions are what we would expect if the sayings really do come from a Jewish rabbi.

Genius: The Golden Rule

In considering whether Jesus said something or not, we should remember that it is simpler to suppose that one genius came up with remarkable teaching than to posit that multiple people had brilliant ideas and all independently attributed them to the same prior teacher.

As an example of this principle, we can consider the so-called Golden Rule. Jesus is reported to have taught, "So whatever you wish that others would do to you, do also to them, for this is the Law and the Prophets" (Matthew 7:12). The parallel in Luke 6:31 says, "And as you wish that others would do to you, do so to them." This is arguably the first articulation in history of the positive Golden Rule—widely regarded as the highest ethical principle. There are earlier statements of a negative Golden Rule—not to do to others what you do not want them to do to you—or of a positive rule of self-interest, where helping others is seen as the best way to benefit oneself. Given the variety of ancient languages and the possibilities of varied translation, the history of the Golden Rule is far from simple.[4] But it does seem that the most explicit and altruistic form of the rule is first attributed to Jesus. The notion that Jesus was the genius who first came up with this brilliant ethic is far simpler than views that multiply geniuses by supposing that the idea was invented by Matthew, Luke, or an unknown third party used by Matthew and Luke. This type of argument works cumulatively as we consider more of the aspects of Jesus's teaching in the Gospels.

Parables

There is no agreement on the exact number of parables in the Gospels, since scholars count differently, but the Synoptic Gospels record over forty, while John is usually thought to

---

4. Among others, negative versions were made by Confucius, five centuries before Jesus, and the Jewish teacher Hillel, one generation before Jesus. Probably several centuries before Jesus, the Indian epic the Mahabharata, showed a positive formulation, "One should also behave towards all creatures as he should towards himself" (*Shanti Parva* 167, accessed March 14, 2018, http://mahabharataonline.com/translation/mahabharata _12a166.php).

contain none. The parables in the Synoptics occur in material unique to Matthew and Luke, in Mark, in the overlap of Matthew and Luke (i.e., Q), and in material contained in all three Gospels. In fact, more parables are attributed to Jesus than to any other ancient rabbi.

There are three reasons why the simplest hypothesis is that Jesus told many of these parables: (1) Though Jewish sources often attribute parables to rabbis, there are few parables in the Old Testament or Dead Sea Scrolls and none in the Apocrypha, and few are used by early Christians outside the New Testament.[5] Parables are a Jewish genre and fit within the period after the Old Testament, but before Christianity became less Jewish in feel. (2) If we want to say that Jesus told *none* of the parables, we need to have at least *three* individuals who created different parables in order to explain those unique to each source. This is problematic when we know that soon afterward, parables were not a popular form for early Christian authors to use. If we suppose that Jesus told *some* of these parables and others were put on his lips by followers, again we have multiple parable tellers at different periods, with parables suddenly going out of fashion among Christians. (3) Some of Jesus's parables, such as the parables of the sower, good Samaritan, and prodigal son, are viewed as masterpieces of composition. It is far simpler to suppose that the founding figure of the new religion was the creative genius for these stories than to suppose that several later creative geniuses all credited their less creative founder with their great compositions.

We may also note how Jesus's parables fit well in the time in which they are set. Rabbi Yohanan ben Zakkai, in the mid-first century, told a parable of a king inviting servants to a

---

5. An example of an early Christian writing somewhat like a parable is the *Shepherd of Hermas*, which probably comes from the second century AD. However, it is unlike the Gospel parables in length and genre.

banquet, some wise and others foolish, the latter of whom did not wear the proper attire, incurring the king's anger.[6] The key elements of the story are found within *two* different parables of Jesus (Matthew 22:1–14; 25:1–13). Jesus's parables, in fact, frequently contain traditional Jewish themes rearranged to make his own, often surprising, conclusions. These motifs, therefore, more probably reflect the Palestinian Judaism of Jesus than the setting of the church decades after its beginning as it came to be more dominated by Gentiles.

Son of Man

We have already seen that the Gospels show interesting naming patterns whereby their main protagonist tends to be called *Jesus* in the narrative and *Jesus* plus a disambiguator in speech. There is, however, a third layer to the pattern, and that is Jesus's own self-designation as *Son of Man*. It is his preferred name, occurring in all four Gospels and in all five main types of material (unique to Matthew,[7] unique to Luke,[8] Matthew-Luke overlapping,[9] Matthew-Mark-Luke,[10] and John[11]). Just as parables were not common after the time of the New Testament, so we find that later Christians do not commonly use the title *Son of Man* to refer to Jesus, other than when quoting the Gospels. It is, therefore, most obvious to see the material calling Jesus "Son of Man" as coming from early sources.

The Difference between John and the Synoptics

We have seen already that the way Jesus is recorded as speaking in John's Gospel is rather different from the way he speaks in

6. Babylonian Talmud *Shabbat* 153a.
7. E.g., Matthew 13:41.
8. E.g., Luke 18:8.
9. E.g., Matthew 8:20; Luke 9:58.
10. E.g., Matthew 9:6; Mark 2:10; Luke 5:24.
11. E.g., John 1:51.

the Synoptic Gospels: in John there are no clear parables, but there is the series of prominent "I am the . . ." sayings with no obvious parallel in the Synoptics. Themes are treated with quite different frequencies, and the whole style of discourse appears dissimilar. This might give rise to a view that one cannot accept both the Johannine and the Synoptic portraits as true.

However, some data suggest that both John and the Synoptics at times draw upon a larger body of common material, which is what common memory would be. For instance:

1. John contains sections where Jesus speaks of his relationship with God as that between Father and Son, and speaks of the closeness of his relationship with the Father as a relationship of "knowing" (e.g., John 10:15; 17:25). Although this sort of language usually has no parallel in the Synoptics, there is an exception in Matthew 11:25–27, which brings together a range of usually Johannine themes. The appearance of such material in Matthew is explained if this was a way Jesus actually spoke and if the absence of such material from Mark and Luke is more a matter of selective presentation than of Jesus not using such language.

2. As noted earlier, both in the Synoptics and in John, Jesus refers to himself as the "Son of Man." It is generally agreed that some of the background of this expression in the Synoptics is from the Old Testament text Daniel 7:13–14, which speaks of one "like a son of man" coming "with the clouds" toward a figure depicted as God on his throne. The one *like a son of man* then receives *authority* or *dominion* and an *everlasting kingdom*. When we look at the "Son of Man" sayings in the Synoptic Gospels, we see at least two themes from Daniel 7 recurring: (a) coming (sometimes, with the clouds, e.g., Mark 14:62), and (b) authority (e.g., Mark 2:10, 28). Benjamin Reynolds has shown that these same themes are more subtly present behind

some of the uses in John.[12] This supports the idea of a common mind, most probably in the form of a common speaker, behind the occurrences in both the Synoptics and John.

3. Matthew and John give different accounts of the resurrection. Matthew writes of the angel rolling away the stone from the tomb, frightening the guards, and addressing the women, who then run away and encounter Jesus. John tells of Mary going to the tomb. At first we might think she is alone, but she returns saying that she and some others do not know where Jesus's body is. Then two disciples run to the tomb. Mary, back again at the tomb, sees two angels, whereupon she turns and sees Jesus, whom she at first mistakes for a gardener. The two accounts are not incompatible when we allow them to be précis (i.e., abridged accounts or abbreviated summaries) of a fuller set of events, especially if we consider the possibility that different Gospel writers recorded what different female witnesses reported to them. After all, the women at the tomb did not have to move in absolute unity. However, despite their differences Matthew and John suddenly converge when the woman or women meet Jesus for the first time.

> And behold, Jesus met them and said, "Greetings!" And they came up and *took hold of his feet* and worshiped him. Then Jesus said to them, "Do not be afraid; go and tell *my brothers* to go to Galilee, and there they will see me." (Matthew 28:9–10)

> Jesus said to her, "*Do not cling to me*, for I have not yet ascended to the Father; but go to *my brothers* and say to them 'I am ascending to *my Father* and *your Father*, to my God and your God.'" (John 20:17)

---

12. Benjamin E. Reynolds, *The Apocalyptic Son of Man in the Gospel of John* (Tübingen: Mohr Siebeck, 2008), 225–26.

Both Matthew and John describe the participants as holding or trying to hold Jesus, after which Jesus instructs them to go and inform "my brothers," seeming to mean his disciples, though that is not Jesus's usual label for his disciples. The speech of Jesus given in John explains the logic of the term, since Jesus and the disciples share a common Father, God.

The fact that the resurrection accounts agree on the major story—the empty tomb and angel(s) seen prior to the encounter with Jesus—differ on many midsized points, and then agree on tiny details such as these, reflects the sort of pattern we would expect from independent reports, not from direct literary dependence or deliberate falsification of narratives. Here the literary evidence suggests that speech has been independently preserved in two witnesses.

In another interesting agreement between Matthew and John, Jesus prays in the garden of Gethsemane that, if possible, he might avoid drinking the "cup" (Matthew 26:39)—a prayer not recorded in John. But in John, at his arrest moments later in the garden, Jesus counters Peter's attempt to intervene in the operation by saying, "Shall I not drink the *cup* that the Father has given me?" (John 18:11).[13] The explanation that Jesus was thinking about the cup (of suffering)[14] and that, therefore, two sources have recorded the very words of Jesus is beautifully simple. Any other explanation will be more complex.

Has Jesus's Teaching Been Corrupted in Translation from Aramaic?

Many theories have been built on the idea that Jesus's teaching was lost in translation. In considering this possibility, we must start with perspective: though translation never completely cor-

---

13. See Lydia McGrew, *Hidden in Plain View: Undesigned Coincidences in the Gospels and Acts* (Chillicothe, OH: DeWard, 2017), 51–53.

14. E.g., Matthew 20:22; or even the cup of God's anger, e.g., Jeremiah 25:15.

responds to the original, and words may often be mistranslated, mistranslation is far less common than correct translation. We do not, therefore, assign the same initial probability to the view that something has been mistranslated as to the view that it has been correctly translated.

The linguistic knowledge of Jesus is debated. There is a long history of viewing Jesus as speaking only in Aramaic, and indeed Mark records Jesus as speaking Aramaic to a little girl (5:41) and to a deaf and mute person (7:34). But the still-popular idea that Palestine was an *exclusively* Aramaic-speaking domain probably owes more to the romance of the idea than to any hard historical evidence. Since the time of Alexander the Great (356–323 BC), Greek influence and language had spread throughout areas he conquered so that, by the time of Jesus, even Jerusalem's ruling Jewish council was called by a Greek name—*Sanhedrin* (Greek, *synedrion*). Jesus came from Nazareth, less than four miles from Sepphoris, which was the capital of Galilee in Jesus's early years. Sepphoris was substantially Jewish, but shows significant outside influence, including a Roman amphitheater.[15] As both Jesus and Joseph, who was at least legally Jesus's father, are described by the Greek term *tektōn*, meaning carpenter or builder,[16] it is likely that they would have been involved in the major construction projects in the area and had interaction with Greek speakers. In fact, it would have been impossible for them to conduct any form of business without handling coins inscribed with Greek writing. Moreover, the majority of funerary texts from Palestine at the time are in Greek. The idea that Jesus could not have spoken Greek is therefore wide open to challenge.

---

15. C. Thomas McCollough, "City and Village in Lower Galilee: The Import of the Archeological Excavations at Sepphoris and Khirbet Qana (Cana) for Framing the Economic Context of Jesus," in *The Galilean Economy in the Time of Jesus*, ed. David A. Fiensy and Ralph K. Hawkins (Atlanta: SBL, 2013), 52.

16. Matthew 13:55; Mark 6:3.

Jesus's sayings actually sometimes reflect Greek word play. Matthew 5–7 records Jesus's most famous sermon, known as the Sermon on the Mount. It opens with the Beatitudes (sayings of blessing) in Matthew 5:3–11. The first four Beatitudes begin with alliteration of *pi* (the Greek letter *p*), while the famous expressions "poor in spirit" (5:3),[17] "thirst for righteousness" (5:6),[18] "pure in heart" (5:8),[19] and "persecuted for righteousness" (5:10)[20] all involve alliteration and assonance, which seem to suggest that Matthew portrays Jesus as teaching (on this occasion) in Greek.

Luke records what appears to be the same sermon differently, beginning with four beatitudes and then four woes (6:20–26). Since Matthew has no woes, Luke obviously did not get the woes from Matthew. Equally clearly, Matthew did not get *all eight* of his beatitudes from Luke's *four*. The evidence suggests, rather, that they both drew on an earlier source that was longer than either Matthew or Luke.

This can be seen by the fact that while the first two beatitudes in Luke's parallel (6:20–21) begin with *pi*, all four of Luke's woes (6:24–26) have alliteration with *pi* and the *p* sound. This suggests that Matthew and Luke accessed a longer source that had more alliteration than either of them shows. This source could, of course, be the original sermon.

The idea that Jesus spoke in Greek for the Sermon on the Mount would, of course, be suitable if the event really took place as recorded, since according to Matthew the crowds that heard him came not only from Galilee, Jerusalem, and Judaea, but also from beyond the Jordan and from the Decapolis—a collection of ten or more cities marked by *Greek* culture (Matthew 4:25).

---

17. A consonant cluster beginning with *pi* in *ptōchoi*, "poor," and *pneuma*, "spirit."
18. The letters *delta* and *iota* in *dipsō*, "thirst," and *dikaiosunē*, "righteousness."
19. The letters *kappa* and *alpha* in *katharos*, "pure," and *kardia*, "heart."
20. The letters *delta* and *iota* in *diōkō*, "persecute," and *dikaiosunē*, "righteousness."

The alliteration also indicates material designed to be memorized.

Now, I am not saying that this indicates that Jesus taught always or mostly in Greek, so much as that, in multilingual settings, complex communication occurs despite the language barrier. Two of Jesus's twelve disciples—Andrew and Philip—had Greek names. They are presented in John 12:20–22 as intermediaries for some Greeks who wanted to see Jesus. Jesus might have taught in Greek or been translated simultaneously into Greek, or might have approved translations of his own sayings into Greek. There are various possibilities.

Also, though Greek and Aramaic are completely different languages, the prolonged contact in Palestine between speakers of these two languages would have ensured that many people understood some of each and that prolonged and repeated misunderstanding would have been relatively rare. Language contact means that a Jew speaking in Greek to a Jewish audience would plausibly be able to use specifically Aramaic words as recorded in Matthew 5:22 (*raka*) and 6:24 (*mamōna*), both of which occur in the Sermon on the Mount. Also, by the time of Jesus many Greek words had been loaned into Aramaic. If Jesus originally told the parable of the prodigal son in Aramaic, there is no reason why he could not have used some of the very vocabulary found in our Greek version, such as the Greek word *symphōnia* ("music," Luke 15:25), which by then had been adopted into Aramaic. Jesus presumably would have spoken Greek with the Greeks in John 12:23, with the centurion in Matthew 8:5–13, with the Greek woman in Mark 7:26, and possibly also with the Herodians in Mark 12:13.[21]

---

21. Stanley E. Porter, *The Criteria for Authenticity in Historical-Jesus Research: Previous Discussion and New Proposals* (Sheffield: Sheffield Academic Press, 2000), 144–54, considers occasions when Jesus may have spoken Greek.

Conclusion

Returning to the question of whether we can trust the Gospels to report accurately Jesus's words, we find many converging reasons to believe that we have content that originated from Jesus. These include the nature of the teaching, the genre (parables), and the levels of verbal agreement between different accounts.

The fact that the Gospels do not have verbatim agreement is not on its own a concern when we consider that the modern rules of bounded quotation did not exist at the time of the Gospels. The view that some, much, most, or even all of Jesus's teaching was done in Aramaic and is only recorded in a translated form in the Greek Gospels is not on its own a sufficient reason to doubt that we have a reliable record of what Jesus said.

6

Has the Text Changed?

As we consider whether we can trust the Gospels, we need to know if they have been reliably transmitted to us. In terms of sheer volume of manuscripts in different languages, the Gospels, or perhaps the biblical Psalms, are the best documented texts from antiquity by some margin. They are also arguably the most scrutinized texts.

Our Gospel manuscripts mostly come from outside of Palestine, from countries such as Egypt, Italy, Greece, or Turkey. We can hardly suppose that scribes in these countries were responsible for introducing accurate Palestinian cultural knowledge into the Gospels. The view, then, that the Gospels have been reliably handed down does not even need the abundant evidence of the manuscripts we have.

It is also worth pointing out that much of the study of classical Greek and Latin literature is built on a foundation that no one really acquainted with Greek and Latin manuscripts doubts, namely, that most such manuscripts from the ninth through to the sixteenth centuries AD give us a reasonable representation of texts as they were in classical Greece or Rome. It is precisely this fact that has allowed Western schools to teach classical literature to children for over half a millennium. Medieval scribes from the Middle East right across to Ireland and Spain had copying classical and biblical texts as one of their main tasks. There were numerous instances of poor copying and some of downright falsification, but the overwhelming majority of scribes performed their job conscientiously, such that we can say that Christian copyists succeeded where the Greeks and the Romans of the classical period did not. Neither the Greeks nor the Romans passed down to subsequent generations the literature of the cultures that preceded them. By contrast, Christian scribes faithfully copied many pagan Greek and Latin authors with scarcely any interference resulting from the beliefs of the copyists. Christian scribes literally saved the pagan literature.

It should also be observed that this competence in copying is not unique to Latin and Greek literature. Arabic, Chinese, Hebrew, Sanskrit, and Syriac texts, to name just a few, have been transmitted by scribes for periods in excess of a millennium with extraordinary accuracy. When assessing an ancient text, we must avoid the trap of assuming that a text is untrustworthy until demonstrated trustworthy. Rather, we may rationally assume that most later manuscripts are reasonable representations of ancient texts.

The Cleverest Man on Earth

In his age, Desiderius Erasmus (1466–1536) was reputedly the world's most learned man, and in 1516 he produced the first published and printed edition of the New Testament in Greek. For the Gospels, he had only two manuscripts available to make the edition. These are now appropriately called manuscript numbers 1 and 2, both from the twelfth century. In other words, there was a gap of over a millennium between Erasmus's manuscripts and the time of the Gospels. Some might think that is a long time during which the text could have changed. But we need to ask whether it actually did.

Since Erasmus's time, around a couple of thousand Greek manuscripts of the Gospels have been discovered or identified. Most are medieval, but some are much earlier than those Erasmus had. We now have two important manuscripts of all four Gospels—Codex Vaticanus and Codex Sinaiticus—from approximately AD 350, both of which became available during the nineteenth century. In the twentieth century, partial manuscripts of all four Gospels from the third century were discovered, especially of John's Gospel. Some of the early fragments of copies of Matthew and John may even come from the second century. In other words, the gap between the earliest available manuscripts and the writing of the Gospels themselves has narrowed massively since Erasmus's day.[1] This has made a difference to our modern translations of the Gospels, but not much of one.

The most noticeable differences between a sixteenth-century copy of the Gospels (whether an *edition* of the original language or *translation* into a modern language) and a modern version of the Gospels relate to twelve verses following Mark 16:8 and twelve verses in John 7:53–8:11. Whereas these verses were included without any indication of doubt about them in editions and translations from the beginning of printing to the nineteenth century, most scholars now believe that these passages are later additions to the Gospels. This is reflected in the

---

1. The authoritative list of Greek New Testament manuscripts is maintained by the Institute for New Testament Textual Research (Institut für Neutestamentliche Textforschung) in Münster and is known as the *Kurzgefaßte Liste* (short list) or just as the *Liste*. The most up-to-date version is maintained online at http://ntvmr.uni-muenster.de/liste.

way they are marked in most modern editions, as well as many modern translations.

These two passages might seem to cast doubt on the text of the Gospels as a whole, but I would argue that they in fact have the opposite effect. Though Erasmus produced his first edition of the Greek Gospels using just two manuscripts, we know that he knew about the uncertainty attached to these two passages. His manuscript number 1 told him of the uncertainty at the end of Mark and also omitted the passage in John. In other words, the most learned man on earth in the sixteenth century would not have been surprised by any discoveries in the last five centuries that have called these verses into question. In fact, doubts about them have been known to anyone who took care to investigate during the last sixteen hundred years.

These two passages, precisely by being doubtful, provide strong arguments for the reliability of the text in the rest of the Gospels. For a start, they show that Gospel manuscripts vary, and therefore there has been no successful attempt by rulers or scribes to make them all agree or to cover up debate. Gospel manuscripts came from many different countries and were made under various jurisdictions. From the second century onward we also have records of numerous people quoting the Gospels. From no later than the third century the Gospels were also translated into other languages: Coptic, Latin, and Syriac; from the fifth century, into Armenian and Gothic; and by the turn of the first millennium, into Anglo-Saxon, Arabic, Georgian, and Old Church Slavonic, among others. In light of this abundance of evidence, the possibility of any major changes taking place without leaving some record in manuscripts somewhere on the globe is remote.

Consider, too, some smaller but still significant differences between Erasmus's edition and most modern Bibles.

Erasmus's editions of the Greek New Testament became the basis for other editions, and the one by the Parisian printer Robert Estienne (Stephanus) in 1551 is justly famous for introducing verse numbers. Those numbers are still used today and provide a simple way of noticing anything that was in Estienne's edition but is not in a modern printing of the Gospels. In total, there are eleven instances where Estienne gave a verse number and a reader of a modern Bible is likely to find no corresponding verse.[2] For instance, in the English Standard Version the verse after Matthew 18:10 is 18:12. Between these two verses older translations had the words "For the Son of Man came to save the lost," which are present in most of the manuscripts but missing in some, including the two earliest and some of the translations into Coptic, Latin, and Syriac. Despite this difference, this and similar matters would not have surprised Erasmus, whose scholarly notes on the New Testament, called *Annotationes* (1527), commented on the uncertainty of three of the eleven verses in question.[3] When we combine these eleven verses with the two twelve-verse passages mentioned above, we see that overall a total of thirty-five verses in Erasmus's 1516 edition of the Gospels have been since called into question. However, on the basis of the much more limited evidence available to him, Erasmus already knew about the uncertainty of the two twelve-verse passages and three of the eleven other verses.

---

2. Such Bibles would include the English Standard Version, New International Version, New Living Translation, and New Revised Standard Version, but not the New King James Version, which adheres closely to the textual content of the 1611 King James Version. There is a widespread popular movement that seeks to maintain the continued superiority of the King James Version and its underlying Greek, known as the *Textus Receptus* (Received Text), which was very close to that of Erasmus.

3. Desiderius Erasmus, *In Novum Testamentum Annotationes* (Basel: Froben, 1527), shows knowledge of the uncertainty surrounding Matthew 18:11 (p. 72); Mark 11:26 (p. 131); and Luke 17:36 (p. 193) but shows no awareness of questions about Matthew 17:21; 23:14; Mark 7:16; 9:44, 46; Luke 23:17, and only limited awareness of textual issues in John 5:4 (p. 227). Of John 7:53–8:11, Erasmus says, "The story of the adulterous woman is not contained in the majority of Greek copies" (p. 234).

That means he knew about the uncertainty in at least twenty-seven out of thirty-five verses, or about 77 percent of them.

We now have nearly a thousand times more manuscripts than were used by Erasmus in his first edition, and as the gap between the earliest discovered manuscripts and the original writings has narrowed by nearly a thousand years, not much has changed. With just a fraction of the information we now have, and with only late manuscripts, Erasmus knew about the most significant textual questions in the Gospels. This suggests that as we discover more and earlier manuscripts and the time gap continues to narrow, there is no reason to assume this will increase our uncertainty about the text of the Gospels. If discoveries in the future are anything like discoveries in the last five hundred years, then we do not expect editions of the Gospels to change much.

Vindication of Trust

All this vindicates scholarly trust in manuscripts. Erasmus combined his fine mind with rational trust in the manuscripts available to him and was able to produce an edition of the Gospels that represented them essentially as they were over a thousand years before his time. The order of the stories and passages in the Gospels is the same. None of the stories changes substantially in meaning. Apart from the two well-known twelve-verse passages, differences are likely only to be noticeable to an attentive reader doing a line-by-line comparison.

The existence of these thirty-five verses in older editions and translations of course casts no doubt upon the rest of the text of the Gospels in modern translations that either omit these verses or mark them as uncertain. If many modern scholars are wrong in thinking that these verses should be omitted, it only means that modern copies of the Gospels might contain *too little*, not too much.[4] In other words, it gives no reason to distrust what is actually there and not marked with doubt.

We should, however, consider a few short passages where some significant manuscripts omit the wording printed in modern editions and some scholars therefore suggest that there is actually *too much* text in modern translations. The cases in point are Matthew 16:2b–3, Luke 22:43–44, and Luke 23:34a—the equivalent of about *four* verses of text, or close to 0.1 percent of New Testament verses. In these cases there are manuscripts that have them and others that omit them, and scholarly opinion is found on both sides of the argument.

From 2007 to 2017, Tyndale House, the biblical research institute I lead, worked on its own edition of the New Testament in Greek. Dr. Dirk Jongkind, Fellow of St Edmund's College, Cambridge University—one of the world's leading experts on studying the mistakes that scribes make—is editor, while I am associate editor. In *The Greek New Testament, Produced at Tyndale House, Cambridge* we conclude that all of this last group of verses are part of the earliest text of the Gospels. However, even if we are wrong, this does not call into question the rest of the Gospel text but, again, simply reinforces the fact that we have many and varied manuscripts, and that no central authority has been able to impose uniformity. Therefore when manuscripts all agree, there is no good reason not to trust that the text has been reliably transmitted.

As we produced our new edition, I took particular charge of ensuring that we spelled Greek words right. *Right* does not mean according to the rules one learns from grammars and

---

4. Though I am not convinced by his case, Maurice Robinson makes a spirited defense of many of these longer forms of the text in the appendix to Maurice A. Robinson and William G. Pierpont, *The New Testament in the Original Greek: Byzantine Textform 2005* (Southborough, MA: Hilton, 2005), 533–86.

dictionaries. *Right* often means spelling a word in a way that would have seemed right to scribes back then, even if it goes against the way we have been taught the language should be. So I started my research with a very open mind about how we might end up spelling Greek, and made notes of many nonconventional spellings found in manuscripts.

In producing our edition, however, we needed to be sure that we were not just printing the oddities of a single scribe. We therefore made a rule that any spelling we printed had to be attested by at least two manuscripts and must not be just something in line with the common mistakes of those manuscripts. We set about editing the New Testament based on the manuscripts known today, but leaning particularly on the methods of detecting scribal mistakes developed by Jongkind and others. We expected that our edition would be rather different from other editions. In scholarly terms, looking at many small details, it *is* different. But when we finally had a scholar and software expert, Dr. Drayton Benner, run quantitative comparisons between our edition and others, he found that the edition we were closest to was the edition made by the German Bible Society in 1979 and reproduced without change in 1993, known as the Nestle-Aland edition.[5] The text is the main one used by scholars worldwide and by Bible translators.[6] In other words, different scholars with divergent scholarly emphases sifting through the same manuscript material reached surprisingly similar conclusions. I know this in my personal experience, because I was one of those scholars.

---

5. The 1979 edition is the 26th, and the 1993 the 27th. The differences are in the front and back matter and the scholarly apparatus, not the main text. There is also now the 28th edition, from 2012, whose text is identical to the other editions in the Gospels, except in spelling.

6. The edition commonly used by Bible translators is that of the United Bible Societies (UBS), but other than in spelling, the text of the Gospels in the UBS 3rd to 5th editions (1975, 1993, 2014) is identical to that in the Nestle-Aland 26th to 28th editions.

We may illustrate this a little further by considering the first fourteen verses of John's Gospel. Five completely different editions have exactly the same words and even letters:

- Erasmus's edition from 1516, made on the basis of two twelfth-century manuscripts;
- the 1979, 1993, and 2012 editions of the German Bible Society, used by most scholars;
- the 2005 edition by Maurice Robinson, who prefers the type of text reflected in the manuscripts of the Byzantine Empire;
- the 2010 edition made by Michael Holmes under the auspices of the Society of Biblical Literature, the largest learned society in the world for the academic study of the Bible and a constituent society of the American Council of Learned Societies;
- the 2017 edition made at my own institution, Tyndale House, Cambridge.

The editions of the German Bible Society, the Society of Biblical Literature, and Tyndale House follow different editorial philosophies in consulting the vast range of material for John's Gospel predating anything available to Erasmus, including two early papyri—Papyrus 66 and Papyrus 75—which are regularly dated to the early third century.[7]

But as we look at these opening fourteen verses of John's Gospel, a sequence of 188 words or 812 letters, we find *no differences* in these editions. Erasmus, on the basis of the manuscripts

---

7. The largest ever project to edit the Greek of a Gospel is called the International Greek New Testament Project or the IGNTP (www.igntp.org). It began in 1948 in order to produce scholarly editions of the New Testament in Greek. Since the late 1980s the IGNTP has been working on an edition of John's Gospel. I have the privilege of chairing the IGNTP, which involves dozens of collaborators and many of the world's top scholars of the New Testament text, though I have to confess that I do not do much of the work. This project has produced the best place to access transcriptions of early manuscripts of John in Greek and other languages: www.iohannes.com.

that just happened to be available to him in Basel, Switzerland, on the eve of the Reformation, was able to do just as well as twenty-first-century scholars who are able to enjoy the fruits of half a millennium of accumulated knowledge. This includes all the manuscripts discovered in all the great libraries and monasteries of Europe and the Middle East and all the early papyri that lay hidden in the sands of Egypt since the time of the Roman Empire. This suggests it is absolutely rational to trust that the text of the Gospels has been passed down the centuries with integrity.

However, I want to pursue this question a little further back.

Could the Text Have Been Changed Early On?

Someone reading this might readily acknowledge that the text of the Gospels has been handed down with substantial integrity since an early period, but he or she might reasonably ask why the text could not have changed *before* our earliest copies. We can address this question at several levels.

First, remember that this book is not about *proving* that the Gospels are true but about demonstrating that they can be rationally trusted. Hopefully, by the end of this book I will have demonstrated that trusting the Gospels is more rational than any of the alternatives. Proof of the mathematical kind does not exist with history.

Second, to prove that something has not changed would be to prove a negative. Proving negatives is often impossible.

Third, it is possible to demonstrate that there is *no good reason* to think that the text has changed. That is what I have sought to do in this chapter.

Fourth, based on the facts I have laid out above, we can see that there are *good reasons* to think it has not changed. That is, if past discoveries are any indication of future discoveries, and if what we currently know about scribes and manuscripts is any guide to what we will find out in the future, we do not expect to find evidence of significant change. It is those who suppose that major change occurred before our earliest manuscripts who are proposing a radical discontinuity between all the centuries we know about and the time immediately before our earliest copies. We might say that they are filling in gaps in the evidence using their imaginations rather than what we already know.

Some might suggest that perhaps at first the books were not sacred and therefore could more easily be changed, and that only once they were sacred was there pressure not to change the text. In fact, skeptical historical scholarship often claims that something was probably not the case until immediately before our earliest witness that it was. But what if Erasmus or others of his age had thought that way? They might have supposed that all sorts of things had changed *just before* their earliest manuscripts, when in fact subsequent discovery has shown that they had not. Someone supposing radical change in the short period between the writing of the Gospels and our earliest manuscripts is therefore at risk of making unevidenced claims of events in a period that is ever reducing as more manuscripts are discovered.

But suppose we think of the decades after the Gospels were completed, perhaps ten, twenty, thirty, or forty years later. Can we imagine someone changing the four Gospels then? This also is difficult, because Christianity was spreading fast. The further the Gospels spread, the harder it would have been for anyone logistically to travel and change everyone's copies. By the final quarter of the second century, the four Gospels were circulating as a collection across a wide area. For a while there must have been some transition during which Gospels circulated both individually—one Gospel without the others—and as a collection of all four. This of course means that anyone wanting to change a Gospel would have had to change it in both media (collected and individual), as well as in a wide range of locations. The scenario of widespread deliberate change starts to become fantastical.

In returning, then, to the question of the trustworthiness of the Gospel text, it is rational to have a high degree of confidence in the text of the Gospels as it appears in modern editions. These editions themselves indicate where uncertainties lie. Any changes to the text from the earliest composition would have to be limited to (1) changes to an individual Gospel, or (2) changes that were small enough to be adopted as authentic by copyists who would not want to have passed on anything they knew was changed, or (3) changes for which there is ongoing evidence in our manuscripts.

One more thing: A lot of copying was done by professional scribes, who were trained and paid simply to replicate faithfully what they had in front of them. The idea that scribes acted as if they were authors or were the source of constant ideological change in texts goes against what we know about scribes from the ancient world.[8]

---

8. Ulrich Schmid, "Scribes and Variants—Sociology and Typology," in *Textual Variation: Theological and Social Tendencies? Papers from the Fifth Birmingham Colloquium on the Textual Criticism of the New Testament*, ed. D. C. Parker and H. A. G. Houghton (Piscataway, NJ: Gorgias, 2008), 1–23.

7

What about Contradictions?

So far we have surveyed various lines of evidence for the trust-worthiness of the Gospel record, but I now want to consider the common complaint of contradictions within the Gospels. A consequence of having four records of the same life is that there are many overlapping sections among accounts and many opportunities for narratives to differ from each other. It is actually common in normal life that multiple reports of the same events will be, or will at least seem to be, in conflict with each other. Over the years, many contradictions have been alleged between the Gospels—this at least suggests a degree of independence within each account.

However, my brief journey into this subject will focus on how the Gospel of John contains many *deliberate formal contradictions* within itself and with other literature (such as the First Letter of John, which shows the same authorial style). Here are some examples.

1. *God loves the world versus do not love the world*

   For God so loved the world, that he gave his only Son, that whoever believes in him should not perish but have eternal life. (John 3:16)

Do not love the world or the things in the world. If anyone loves the world, the love of the Father is not in him. (1 John 2:15)

2. *People believed when they saw Jesus's signs versus they did not believe*

Now when he was in Jerusalem at the Passover Feast, many believed in his name when they saw the signs that he was doing. (John 2:23)

Though he had done so many signs before them, they still did not believe in him. (John 12:37)

3. *They know Jesus and where he comes from versus they do not*

So Jesus proclaimed, as he taught in the temple, "You know me, and you know where I come from." (John 7:28)

Jesus answered, "Even if I do bear witness about myself, my testimony is true, for I know where I came from and where I am going, but you do not know where I come from or where I am going." (John 8:14)

They said to him therefore, "Where is your Father?" Jesus answered, "You know neither me nor my Father. If you knew me, you would know my Father also." (John 8:19)

4. *If Jesus bears witness of himself, his testimony is not true, versus the opposite*

If I bear witness about myself, my testimony is not true. (John 5:31, my trans.)

So the Pharisees said to him, "You are bearing witness about yourself; your testimony is not true." Jesus answered, "Even if I do bear witness about myself, my testimony is true, for I know where I came from and where I am going, but you do not know where I come from or where I am going." (John 8:13–14)

5. *Jesus judges no one versus he has much to judge*

You judge according to the flesh; I judge no one. (John 8:15)

Yet even if I do judge, my judgment is true, for it is not I alone who judge, but I and the Father who sent me. (John 8:16)

I have much to say about you and much to judge, but he who sent me is true, and I declare to the world what I have heard from him. (John 8:26)

6. *Jesus did not come into the world to judge it versus he came to judge*

If anyone hears my words and does not keep them, I do not judge him; for I did not come to judge the world but to save the world. (John 12:47)

For God did not send his Son into the world to condemn the world, but in order that the world might be saved through him. (John 3:17)

Jesus said, "For judgment I came into this world, that those who do not see may see, and those who see may become blind." (John 9:39)

I hope that after reading the list above and studying the subtle way the Gospel of John is written, you will agree that these formal contradictions are deliberate. They are part of the author's way of making us reflect more deeply on the multiple meanings of the words involved.[1] This sample prepares us to

---

1. Oxford philosopher Thomas W. Simpson argues that the formal contradiction of John 5:31 and 8:14 in fact shows "philosophical sophistication." See his "Testimony in

consider a quotation by skeptic Bart Ehrman from a book in which he explains what he thinks are the clearest contradictions within the Gospels:

> One of my favorite apparent discrepancies—I read John for years without realizing how strange this one is—comes in Jesus' "Farewell Discourse," the last address that Jesus delivers to his disciples, at his last meal with them, which takes up all of chapters 13 to 17 in the Gospel according to John. In John 13:36, Peter says to Jesus, "Lord, where are you going?" A few verses later Thomas says, "Lord, we do not know where you are going" (John 14:5). And then, a few minutes later, at the same meal, Jesus upbraids his disciples, saying, "Now I am going to the one who sent me, yet none of you asks me, 'Where are you going?'" (John 16:5). Either Jesus had a very short attention span or there is something strange going on with the sources for these chapters, creating an odd kind of disconnect.[2]

This forms part of Ehrman's cumulative case for there being irreconcilable contradictions within the Gospels. However, it also shows a weakness in his method. In every case listed above, Jesus is portrayed as speaking one or both sides of the contradiction. But why may an outstanding teacher not use paradox? Each of the formal contradictions we have seen highlights the multiple meanings of words. In the Gospel of John, Jesus is going to the cross and then to his Father, God. The disciples are not asking about that but are only thinking in mundane terms of where he will next walk to. Ehrman has just missed the irony.

The problem seems, therefore, to be that the question of contradictions has become part of a point-scoring exercise

John's Gospel: The Puzzle of 5:31 and 8:14," *Tyndale Bulletin* 65, no. 1 (2014): 101–18, esp. 101.

2. Bart D. Ehrman, *Jesus, Interrupted: Revealing the Hidden Contradictions in the Bible (and Why We Don't Know about Them)* (New York: HarperOne, 2009), 9.

between those who claim or deny error in the Gospels. Here the author of John's Gospel has recorded *contradictions at the superficial level of language* to encourage the audience to think more deeply. It is somewhat similar to how Dickens opened his *A Tale of Two Cities* with a whole list of contradictions to characterize the inconsistencies of an era. He famously began, "It was the best of times, it was the worst of times."[3]

The presence of such *deliberate formal contradictions* does not mean that the contradictory statements are not both true in some way at a deeper level. But these formal contradictions do show that the author is more interested in encouraging people to read deeply than in satisfying those who want to find fault.

If one author may use vocabulary in more than one way, why may not two authors? If anyone wants to argue that two Gospel accounts are in such conflict that both cannot be true, he must first ensure that he has correctly understood the claims being made in each text and that he is not reading either of the accounts in a way that is not intended. For all the many contradictions that have been alleged in the Gospels, and for all the texts that remain puzzling, I do not know of any that cannot possibly be resolved.

---

3. Charles Dickens, *A Tale of Two Cities* (London: Chapman & Hall, 1859).

8

Who Would Make
All This Up?

There are many particulars in the Gospels that the authors would be unlikely to have invented. Although one can usually think of complex reasons why someone *might* invent them, those are not the simplest explanations. The simplest explanation is that these reports are true.

The most obvious example is the shameful death of Jesus through crucifixion, which of course was the Romans' way of showing that they were in charge and the one crucified was a defeated failure. However, the Gospel writers record this event and many others that could seem embarrassing to their cause. All four Gospels tell of the leading disciple, Peter, three times denying that he knew Jesus. In all four Gospels the disciples are portrayed as lacking understanding and as disloyal at the key moment of Jesus's arrest.

It is hard to envisage why either the disciples themselves or anyone who looked to them for leadership would make up such stories. It is also hard to see why anyone would write a Gospel that implies its dependence on the disciples for information and then invent such things about them. And this is not the limit of the difficulty. Passages critical of disciples are found in different sorts of Gospel material.[1] For the core texts of Christianity to contain so much material critical of the first Christian leaders is unusual when considered against other religious or political movements. A simple interpretation is that the critical accounts of early leaders signal the trustworthiness of the sources.

What about Miracles?

Undoubtedly the biggest problem for many people in accepting the Gospels as historically trustworthy is that they contain so many miracles. If miracles do not happen today, why should we accept that they happened back then? For some critics, the situation may be summed up in the famous words of Sherlock Holmes: "How often have I said to you that when you have eliminated the impossible, whatever remains, however improbable, must be the truth?"[2] Miracles are impossible, so the argument goes. Therefore, historical reconstructions without miracles, however improbable they may seem, must be correct.

For instance, if we assume atheistic materialism (physical things are all there is), then of course miracles, as understood by Christians, are impossible. No amount of testimony to the contrary would ever be able to mount an acceptable argument to the contrary. Sometimes Christian arguments for miracles are held to that standard and, of course, are found wanting. But the problem is that the atheistic materialistic universe has been taken as a starting point. The premise generates the conclusion.

But when Christians argue for the reality of Gospel miracles, they do not normally hang their entire argument for the truth

---

1. E.g. Matthew 14:28–31; Luke 8:45; 9:55; John 13:8; 18:10.
2. Arthur Conan Doyle, *The Sign of Four* (London: Spencer Blackett, 1890), 111.

of Christianity upon miracles alone. They believe that we live in a universe that shows signs of being made, and that the converging lines of evidence for the truth of Christianity include arguments from the nature of the message, the moral realism of the biblical story, the fulfillment of prophecy, the coherence of the Bible, the need for a source of moral absolutes, the seeming purposefulness of life and nature, their own experience, and more. Whether or not these arguments are valid would require other books to explore. But the point is that *prior convictions* about the nature of the universe shape whether we believe that miracles are possible, let alone probable.[3]

If you are overwhelmingly convinced of materialist atheism, then it is hard to imagine what amount of evidence would persuade you to believe in a random and meaningless miracle, a mere anomaly to your worldview. Of course, those who hold Christ to be the Son of God are arguing not for odd and anomalous miracles but for ones that form a meaningful pattern. However, there is no doubt that Gospel miracles will seem more plausible if you are already rationally convinced that God exists, has performed miracles in the history of Israel, and has prophetically promised a future Messiah.

Carl Sagan famously popularized the phrase "Extraordinary claims require extraordinary evidence,"[4] a favorite line of so-called skeptics to suggest that there is insufficient evidence to believe in biblical miracles. The problem with this seemingly obvious saying is that "extraordinary" is not defined. For an atheist, believing in Gospel miracles is extraordinary. For many

---

3. Michael P. Levine, "Philosophers on Miracles," in *The Cambridge Companion to Miracles*, ed. Graham H. Twelftree (Cambridge: Cambridge University Press, 2011), 292, says, "Few philosophers argue that miracles are impossible, and those who do are in effect presupposing or else arguing for a thoroughgoing naturalism."

4. The problems of this maxim are demonstrated in David Deming, "Do Extraordinary Claims Require Extraordinary Evidence?," *Philosophia* 44, no. 4 (December 2016): 1319–31.

believers in God, the belief that living things arose spontaneously from nonliving things is equally hard to swallow, as is the belief that conscious things arose from nonconscious things, two ideas that many atheists have little difficulty accepting. The question of whether the beliefs of the Christian or the atheist on these matters are rational cannot be considered here, but one point may be made.

When most self-designating skeptics accept the belief that life first arose from nonliving matter or that consciousness arose from nonconsciousness by purely material means, with no supernatural superintendence, they hold that these positions need only to reach the normal bar of evidence, not some *extraordinarily high* bar of evidence. The human race divides over whether miracles are possible as it does over whether a wholly materialistic account of origins is possible, with the majority of humanity seeming to side with belief in miracles against the hardcore materialist accounts. For those on either side of this divide to ask the other group to provide "extraordinary evidence" for their beliefs risks circular reasoning.

A further objection to miracles is that they disrupt the orderliness of scientific explanations, but this objection fails to recognize a regular feature of biblical miracles: they are presented not as random disturbances of an otherwise orderly universe but as events that actually form an orderly pattern pointing to God's meaningful action in the world. Reports of miracles surrounding Jesus are not disruptions of order but signs pointing to who he is.

Evidence for the Resurrection of Jesus

The argument of this book has been that the Gospels display signs that would normally be taken as indications of reliability. To make this argument, I have largely ignored the topic of miracles until this chapter. We may put the conclusion so far like this: were it not for the many miraculous reports in the Gospels, most historians would be very happy to treat their accounts as generally historically reliable. This in itself is no small thing. I now want us to consider these narratives *including* their miracles.

If someone is committed to a materialist atheist position on miracles, then no amount of evidence will be able to disturb this belief. He or she will encounter the lines of evidence presented in this book and will find alternative explanations. I believe that these alternative explanations will be complex, involving appeals to numerous scenarios normally judged to be improbable, whereas accepting the historical reliability of the Gospels will be simple.

For those who are not thus constrained, however, the resurrection of Jesus can provide a further line of argumentation for accepting the reliability of the Gospels. Many books argue for the historicity of the resurrection,[5] so I will be very brief as I lay out a case for accepting it.

We may begin with two facts generally accepted even by those who doubt the resurrection: (1) that Jesus was buried and that the tomb was later found empty;[6] (2) that a wide range of people believed that they had seen Jesus risen from the dead.

We establish the empty tomb on the basis of the extremely strong evidence for the importance of burial, even of convicted criminals, among Jews and the focus on the empty tomb within the Gospels and other early Christian traditions. To this we may add the thought that it is hard to imagine belief in a risen Jesus

---

5. See especially N. T. Wright, *The Resurrection of the Son of God* (London: SPCK, 2003).

6. For evidence that even someone who had been crucified would not be left unburied by Jews, see Craig A. Evans, *Jesus and the Remains of His Day: Studies in Jesus and the Evidence of Material Culture* (Peabody, MA: Hendrickson, 2015), 109–20, 131–45.

getting very far if one could easily point to the grave in which he was still present.

We establish the idea that a wide range of people believed they had seen Jesus risen from the dead, not only in the Gospel accounts, which focus on the visit of women to the tomb, even though women's testimony was not legally acceptable,[7] but also in the overall variety of claimed resurrection appearances within the New Testament. The resurrected Jesus is recorded as appearing in Judaea[8] and in Galilee,[9] in town[10] and countryside,[11] indoors[12] and outdoors,[13] in the morning[14] and in the evening,[15] by prior appointment[16] and without prior appointment,[17] close[18] and distant,[19] on a hill[20] and by a lake,[21] to groups of men[22] and groups of women,[23] to individuals[24] and groups of up to five hundred,[25] sitting,[26] standing,[27] walking,[28] eating,[29] and *always* talking.[30] Many are explicitly close-up encounters involving conversations. It is hard to imagine this pattern of appearances in the Gospels and early Christian letters

---

7. Josephus, *Antiquities* 4.219.
8. Matthew 28:9; Luke 24:31, 36.
9. Matthew 28:16–20; John 21:1–23.
10. Luke 24:36.
11. Luke 24:15.
12. Luke 24:36.
13. Matthew 28:9, 16; Luke 24:15; John 21:1–23.
14. John 21:1–23.
15. Luke 24:29, 36; John 20:19.
16. Matthew 28:16.
17. Matthew 28:9; Luke 24:15, 34, 36; John 21:1–23.
18. Matthew 28:9, 18; Luke 24:15, 36; John 21:9–23.
19. John 21:4–8.
20. Matthew 28:16.
21. John 21:4.
22. John 21:2; 1 Corinthians 15:5, 7.
23. Matthew 28:9.
24. Luke 24:34; 1 Corinthians 15:5, 7 (and 8).
25. 1 Corinthians 15:6.
26. John 21:15 (implied).
27. John 21:4.
28. Luke 24:15; John 21:20–22.
29. Luke 24:43; John 21:15.
30. Matthew 28:9–10, 18–20; Luke 24:17–30, 36–49; John 20:15–17, 19–29; 21:6–22.

without there having been multiple individuals who claimed to have seen Jesus risen from the dead.

On their own, these two lines of argumentation would produce strong evidence for something exceptional. The empty tomb could be explained in terms of some people having removed the body, which would have been bizarre, but might have been part of a strategic deceit by a small number. Yet that would not explain the many claims by different people to have seen Jesus risen from the dead. The combination of the empty tomb and the resurrection appearances together would make for a very good "whodunnit."

However, we may add further lines of argumentation, which create further problems for those who seek to explain the data without appeal to a miracle.

One can make a good argument that the concept of the bodily resurrection of *one person* in advance of others would have been very odd within Judaism, and therefore it is unlikely that early Christians would have invented it in an effort to continue the Jesus movement after the death of their leader.[31]

Moreover, the reports of the empty tomb and of the resurrection appearances were not of a random person but of someone who would have been an exceptional individual by all accounts. He is credited with more miracles than any other rabbi, with the first version of the positive Golden Rule, with some exceedingly popular stories, with a family line going back to King David,[32] and with membership of arguably the world's most remarkable

---

31. Wright, *Resurrection of the Son of God*, 413.

32. The Davidic genealogy seems to have been legally real. The second-century writer Hegesippus reported that two grandsons of Jesus's brother Judas (Jude) confirmed their Davidic descent during a trial before Domitian (emperor, AD 81–96). See Eusebius, *Ecclesiastical History* 3.20. Genealogy was important for Jews, and public written records of genealogies were kept, at least for priests (Josephus, *Life* 6; Josephus, *Against Apion* 1.31). M. Avi-Yonah, "A List of Priestly Courses from Caesarea," *Israel Exploration Journal* 12, no. 2 (1962): 137–39, discusses an inscription showing that, at least after the time of Jesus, Nazareth was a priestly village. Luke 1:5 and 36 say that Jesus's mother Mary was related to a descendant of the priest Aaron.

ethnic group;[33] and he seems to have been executed by the Romans for his claim to be king of the Jews, and just happened to die (even according to non-Christian sources) at Passover time,[34] just when the Jews celebrated their greatest deliverance—out of Egypt. More coincidences could be added. However, there comes a point when rather than thinking that the miracles attributed to Jesus would *spoil* the pattern of a tidy mechanistic universe, one begins to think that they actually *form* a pattern. One can seek to explain away each phenomenon individually, but a single and simple explanation can make sense of all the facts.

Jesus—the Simpler Explanation

John's Gospel opens, "In the beginning was the Word, and the Word was with God, and the Word was God" (1:1). It is subsequently explained that this Word "became flesh" (1:14) and is in fact "Jesus Christ" (1:17). Here "the Word," which in Greek philosophy could be an abstract creative principle and in Jewish language could be a way of speaking of God himself, is said to be something that has always existed, is God, and yet is distinct from God. All this comes within a Jewish conceptual framework where there is only one God. The Word comes to earth and does what words do—they communicate. The Word tells us who God is.

This presentation of Jesus as the one who tells us who God is can be found in the Synoptic Gospels too. They all present

---

33. According to http://www.jinfo.org/Nobel_Prizes.html, accessed March 14, 2018, those with half or more Jewish ancestry account for 23 percent of individual Nobel Prize recipients.

34. Babylonian Talmud *Sanhedrin* 43a. Colin J. Humphreys and W. G. Waddington, "Dating the Crucifixion," *Nature* 306 (1983): 743–46, argue that the most likely date for the crucifixion is April 3, AD 33. Independent of their argument for this date, they note that there would have been a lunar eclipse, with blood red moon, visible from Jerusalem as people sat down to eat their Passover meal that night—a fact the New Testament never explicitly comments on, but which Peter's first speech in Acts 2:20 may allude to as Peter quotes the uncannily apt prophecy of Joel 2:31 about the moon turning to blood as one of the signs of salvation in Jerusalem.

the thought that God sent his Son to show us who God is and to give up his life to save people (Matthew 20:28; Mark 10:45; Luke 19:10; 22:20). Accepting the Gospels' own presentation of Jesus actually provides the best single explanation for a whole range of phenomena in the Gospels that would otherwise require complicated explanations.

If the presentation of Jesus in the Gospels is wrong, one faces many intellectual hurdles to explain why so many historical details are right or plausible. One has to explain how the various layers of textual material arose in the Gospels, all of which display signs of abundant familiarity with the time of Jesus and show the features one would expect from the earliest Jewish layers of tradition. One needs to explain the origin of the parables, the original teaching, and the range of cases where one Gospel is most simply explained by assuming the truth of another. One also has to explain how the movement of Jesus's followers took off numerically in a manner for which historians cannot agree on an explanation.

I do not want to suggest for a moment that all this cannot be explained away. Humans are ingenious, and therefore, of course, they can explain away anything. In fact, a significant section of professional biblical studies has been relatively successful in providing explanations for each of the isolated phenomena mentioned in this book. However, that could be more an indication of high levels of human ingenuity than of the correctness of these explanations.

Returning to the title of this book, *Can We Trust the Gospels?*, I would argue that it is rational to do so. Trusting both the message and the history of the Gospels provides a satisfying choice both intellectually and in wider ways. Trusting the Gospels has explanatory power historically and literarily, but if the Gospels' presentation is correct in characterizing humans as opposed to God and sinful, the Gospels also provide the answer to these problems in the record of the life, teaching, death, and resurrection of the remarkable person Jesus Christ.

It is noteworthy that in addition to the patterns dealt with so far, the record of Jesus within the Gospels also forms a pattern with the Old Testament—all of which was clearly composed before Jesus lived on earth. Throughout history, Christians have read the Old Testament as prefiguring Jesus Christ in ways that would take many other books for us to explore.

The Old Testament begins with the story of a perfect creation spoiled by human sin, and the consequent death penalty on humans and expulsion from God's presence. Death is the punishment for sin, blood is sacred, sacrifice is needed, and it is promised that a future "seed" (i.e., offspring) will deliver. Abraham, the man God specially privileges, has a special son against all expectation and is told to offer him as a sacrifice, but this is called off at the last moment and the son lives on, being replaced by a ram. Abraham's descendants spend time oppressed in Egypt and are rescued from there, but not before they have sacrificed lambs and put their blood on their doorposts to protect them from God's judgment. Out of Egypt they experience God's presence in their midst in a special tent, a presence to which all their access comes through sacrifice. Within the Promised Land they are given King David, who is promised a "seed" (2 Samuel 7:12 KJV) who will always be on his throne. A culture in which there is only one God speaks boldly through its prophets of a "mighty God" being born (Isaiah 9:6; compare 10:21), of God being pierced and mourned for (Zechariah 12:10), of One spoken of in terms only ever applied to God (Isaiah 52:13) as dying[35] and yet thereafter living (Isaiah 53:11–12).

---

35. "Slaughter" (Isaiah 53:7); "cut off out of the land of the living" (53:8); "his grave" and "his death" (53:9). For evidence that the figure is spoken of in divine language, see Richard Bauckham, *Jesus and the God of Israel: "God Crucified" and Other*

These things and many others map well onto the life, sacrificial death and subsequent resurrection of Jesus, not just in the eyes of devoted believers, but also in the eyes of those skeptical of the Gospels' historicity, who use the high level of correspondence between the story of Jesus and the Old Testament to argue that much of the Gospels' narrative of Jesus was invented on the basis of the Old Testament.[36] For those unfamiliar with the Old Testament or the Gospels, the above list of correspondences may seem like dreamy thinking, but in fact the existence of large-scale correlation between the Gospels' records of Jesus and the Old Testament is something on which a wide range of scholars agree, even while they differ on many specific points of interpretation.

I want, therefore, to take this correspondence as a given. Clearly one option is to use this correspondence as a ground to suggest that early Christians invented the Gospel stories on the basis of the Old Testament. The problem is that this model lacks the power to explain many patterns we have already considered, including undesigned coincidences, the high levels of knowledge of local culture, the existence of parables, the genius of Jesus's teaching, the careful differentiation between speech and narrative, and more. Either Jesus intended to die, in which case he probably already saw himself in the Old Testament narrative, or his death was a miscalculation, in which case any loyal followers wanting to make a successful message out of his death were extremely lucky to have such preexisting material

---

Studies on the New Testament's Christology of Divine Identity (Milton Keynes: Paternoster, 2008), 32–59.

36. For example, atheist Richard Carrier, *On the Historicity of Jesus: Why We Might Have Reason for Doubt* (Sheffield: Sheffield Phoenix, 2014), 84–85, sees the correspondence between the Old Testament book of Daniel and the AD 30 date for Jesus's crucifixion as such a convenient "coincidence" that he regards the year of the crucifixion as "fudged or fabricated." Carrier and I frequently agree on the high levels of correspondence between the Old Testament and Jesus, but whereas I see this as evidence for real prophecy, Carrier sees this as evidence against the historicity of the alleged fulfillment.

in the Old Testament ready to be adapted into a message of a divine Savior rescuing the world through a sacrificial death from which he somehow came back.

A far easier position is to make a single supposition, that all of history hangs on Jesus. It is a single and simple supposition, but I am not claiming that it is a small one.[37] It does have huge explanatory power as it accounts for the signs in the Gospels that would normally be taken as signs of reliability, for the genius of Jesus's character and teaching, for the evidence for the resurrection, and for the correspondence of Jesus's life with the Old Testament. Of course, if Jesus is the Word who is coeternal with God, and the one who has come to save the world, then the question of the trustworthiness of the Gospels is not a mere issue of historical interest. If the picture of Jesus in the Gospels is basically true, it logically demands that we give up possession of our lives to serve Jesus Christ, who said repeatedly in every Gospel, "Follow me."

---

37. For arguments that we should prefer simpler explanations, including in areas of personal explanation, see Richard Swinburne, *Simplicity as Evidence of Truth* (Milwaukee: Marquette University Press, 1997), esp. 57–58.

General Index

Scripture Index